D0347331

Litt

Return items to **any** Swindon Library by closing
time on or before the date stamped. Only books
and Audio Books can be renewed - phone your
library or visit our website,
www.swindon.gov.uk/libraries

NORTH SWINDON LIBRARY
TEL: 707120

18/11/06.
10/12/06.
4-6-09

26/6
WITHDRAWN
06/09/19

6 484 744 000

Copying recordings is illegal. All recorded items
are hired entirely at hirer's own risk

Swindon BOROUGH COUNCIL

Little Big Goals Results

Achieve 100% results with
the 10% approach

Eileen Mulligan

PIATKUS

Visit the Piatkus website!

Piatkus publishes a wide range of best-selling fiction and non-fiction, including books on health, mind, body & spirit, sex, self-help, cookery, biography and the paranormal.

If you want to:

- read descriptions of our popular titles
- buy our books over the internet
- take advantage of our special offers
- enter our monthly competition
- learn more about your favourite Piatkus authors

VISIT OUR WEBSITE AT: www.piatkus.co.uk

**Swindon Borough Council
Library Services**

Askews	
158.1	£9.99

Copyright © 2006 by Eileen Mulligan

First published in Great Britain in 2006 by
Piatkus Books Ltd
5 Windmill Street, London WIT 2JA
email: info@piatkus.co.uk

The moral right of the author has been asserted

A catalogue record for this book is available from the British Library

ISBN 0 7499 2546 9

Text design by Paul Saunders

This book has been printed on paper manufactured
with respect for the environment using wood from
managed sustainable resources

Printed and bound in Great Britain by
Antony Rowe Ltd, Chippenham, Wiltshire

Contents

Introduction   1

Part 1

1. Goals and goal setting   7
2. Changing for the better   26
3. Discovering the real you   38
4. Bringing out the best in you   49
5. Boosting your confidence and self-esteem   61
6. Why it has to be today   77
7. How to have a charmed life   92

Part 2

8. Organising your personal environment   112
9. Looking and feeling great   124
10. Organising your money   139
11. Being happy and successful at work   153
12. Making the most of family relationships   170
13. Building solid friendships   184
14. Improving your personal relationships   201
15. Living, loving and learning   223

Conclusion   240
Index   246

Acknowledgements

Thank you to the fabulous team at Piatkus and Alison Sturgeon my editor for her support, enthusiasm and patience.

Thanks to Nick Morgan for his huge input helping me write this book, providing just the right amount of cajoling and being a terrific sounding-board.

Thanks to my darling little boy Patrick for unplugging my computer if I spent too much time in the study, and to my family and friends for all their love and support.

And finally a massive thank you to my clients whose contribution and feedback made this book possible.

Introduction

TRULY EFFECTIVE SELF-HELP is time enhancing, not time consuming. If you're willing to make a 10 per cent contribution to trying a new approach, then I'll show you how to achieve 100 per cent results. Through a process of setting little goals on a daily basis, you'll discover just how easy it is to turn your life around and achieve the big results you've always wanted.

By reading this book you have signalled to yourself that there's something you want to improve. It could be your health, a work-related problem or a personal relationship. Perhaps it's a general upgrade and a more focused sense of direction you're after. Whatever the reason, I'm very pleased to have the opportunity to work with you. So let's begin with how the 10 per cent approach will change your life.

We all have goals, but it can be easy to lose sight of them, especially if you are battling with a busy schedule. Great achievers recognise their own pace. They make an effort to improve on a daily basis, and know that the key to success is consistency. Trying to do too much in one go is counterproductive, because it's the fastest way to burn out. However, here's the good news: when your focus is directed and your expectations are aligned with your values, time has a wonderful knack of playing ball.

I often explain the 10 per cent approach to my clients by

giving them the analogy of a marathon runner. What these athletes do takes training and dedication, and mental and physical stamina. To achieve their goal they need an excellent training programme that is adapted to their individual requirements. That's what I'm going to provide you with. I will work with you as your personal coach and deliver a training programme that will fit into the busiest schedule. You'll discover how little goals encourage you to think big. That was certainly the case for Daphne Belt.

Case study

At the age of fifty, Daphne weighed over 11 stone – and was just 5 feet 2 inches tall. 'I couldn't climb the stairs without difficulty,' she says. Although she had never been sporty, she joined a gym with the hope of losing weight, but felt dispirited when she failed to keep up with even the easiest programme. Still determined to get fit, she started jogging – very slowly at first. After a month her husband Steve taught her to swim the front crawl. Then she changed her diet, introducing lots of fruit and vegetables and reducing the fat content of her food.

After a year of taking small steps, Daphne entered (and completed) a 10-mile run. That was just the start. She progressed to her first triathlon, which was followed by an Iron Man event (a 2.5-mile open-water swim, a 112-mile cycle and a full 26.2-mile marathon run). Since then she has picked up world titles in the 50–55, 55–60 and 60–65 age groups. Quite an achievement.

How had Daphne been so successful? While taking a series of small and manageable steps, she'd fallen in love with fitness, good diet and exercise. She took on minor hurdles and then steadily worked her way up to the bigger challenges. That's exactly the method I will be using with you in this book: take careful small steps and before you know it you will be scaling a mountain.

I'm an enthusiastic student of life, so settling for less than the best simply won't do. Believe me, I'm very familiar with both struggle and life in the mediocre lane.

I vividly recall growing up in a household where low expectations were the norm. I grew up on a coal-board estate where my mother, two sisters and myself used to cower in a bedroom to keep out of my father's way when he was in a drunken rage. He would gamble on the horses and lose most of his weekly wage, leaving my mother to run the household on a shoestring. Thank goodness she was thrifty as well as loving.

School was no escape for me. I struggled in every subject and walked away from my secondary modern gates with a couple of exam passes and a report that read: 'Eileen finds it difficult to grasp information and concentrate on any subject.' I was convinced that I was destined for the career scrap heap. It seemed impossible to escape my circumstances without a major transformation. That's exactly what I set about achieving, very slowly and step by step – transforming my life in every conceivable way.

Fifteen years later I was running a successful company that clearly had promise. A year after that I was hanging a certificate on the wall, and under my name it said 'Entrepreneur of the Year'. Six months later it was joined by another certificate, this time the prestigious Gucci Business Age award (previously awarded to Richard Branson). My business success lead to Carlton TV featuring me in their documentary about self-made millionaires. I was invited to speak at universities and business schools, to share the secrets of my success. So you can see, it's hardly surprising that I'm such a passionate advocate of the phenomenal potential we all have to transform our lives.

How did I change? The process first began by very simply altering my expectations of what was possible. This small step of self-belief was the beginning of a huge journey towards change – a journey that I will be taking you on. I'll introduce you to the role models that influenced my life, the mentors who imparted wisdom, my clients and their inspiring case histories.

Many people want to change their lives, but the means to take effective action elude them. In my experience this has little to do with a lack of commitment, willingness to work hard, or desire to learn and grow. I often find that clients feel despondent because of their lack of progress in the past. What I always say to them, and will also now say to you, is that my role is to make your life easier. In order to do that I'm going to make change feel like a natural and comfortable process.

It's human nature to want to stay with what's familiar, even if what's familiar isn't favoured. Shifting out of your comfort zone is therefore by no means an easy thing to do. Attempt to do it too quickly and it can be very disappointing to find yourself reverting back to negative or old patterns of behaviour.

Let's say, for example, that you have a very negative body image. What I can tell you for sure is that you won't have formed that opinion today. The chances are that you have been reinforcing that message in your mind for quite some time. With the techniques and exercises I will give you, you won't be expected to feel 100 per cent better about yourself overnight. The goal will be to feel 10 per cent better. Obviously it follows that if we keep working together every day to make you feel 10 per cent better, in 10 days time you'll feel 100 per cent better – and of course we don't have to stop after 10 days.

What if you want to make lots of changes in your life? Surely making a lot of changes will take up a lot of your day? The answer is no, it won't take up a lot of time in your day. In fact, it will only take up 10 per cent of your day. Just five or six minutes out of every hour in your day focusing on how you can do things in a positive way, make a situation work for you and take an action that will move you towards achieving a goal will transform every aspect of your life.

I can already hear you saying, 'Hang on a minute – it can't be that easy' or 'I always try to do things in a positive way.' Firstly, it really is that easy, and secondly, life can cloud our judgement. However keen a student you are, it's important to remember that our ability to learn and change is always hampered by preconceived ideas, especially the ideas we have about ourselves. So if you think, deep down, that people like you don't achieve goals, that you want to change but don't know how, and that you'll have more time or confidence in the future, we'll be eliminating those limiting beliefs in the first half of the book.

In part one I show you how to set goals, what you need to get started, and how to discover the real you and bring out the best in you. I show you how to boost your confidence and achieve indestructible self-esteem, why there's no time like the present and how to take control of your time. At the end of part one you'll discover what I call the five charms, which are simple and practical techniques to create a charmed life.

In part two you will work on creating a harmonious living environment. This part is really practical, and deals with achieving goals in the seven main areas of your life. We get to work on your health, finances and career. Then we move on to family relationships, friendships and affairs of the heart in those close personal relationships. Finally, we reflect on your spiritual path in the role of living, loving and learning.

The techniques I use have worked for my clients across the board. I've coached people from a diverse range of backgrounds, from MPs, celebrities, managing directors, medical professionals, office workers and manual labourers to mothers returning to work after long career breaks and individuals facing major life crises.

I ask my clients to make the simple adjustment that I have requested from you – 10 per cent of every hour of your day. Here are some examples of how this works in practice.

Imagine yourself in the following situations: you're getting ready for work in the morning and instead of grabbing a quick cup of coffee you spend five or six minutes thinking about what would be a better start to your day. So instead of a coffee you drink some water and eat a healthy breakfast like muesli or porridge. You're slumped in front of the TV and could easily spend a few hours watching nothing in particular, but instead you apply the 10 per cent approach and spend five or six minutes deciding how you could put your time to better use.

You also learn how to take credit for your daily achievements. When I ask clients about their greatest achievements in life, they usually have no problem telling me. Yet when I ask them 'What have you achieved today?' the common response is 'Nothing really' or 'Not much.' One high-flying client confessed, 'You've caught me on one of those average days; we all have them.' Well, I beg to differ. Life is too precious to have average days. There are triumphs to be had in every single day – and if that hasn't been your experience so far, it soon will be.

We are about to go back to basics. We will get you focused on what a wonderful, unique individual you are, someone who believes in you, the person you are today and the person you intend to be tomorrow. I'll support you every step of the way, and as you progress through each chapter your confidence, motivation and all-round enthusiasm for life will flourish. Between us, we will ensure that the transformation is fun and truly enlightening.

I'm looking forward to working with you and helping you to make your dreams into a reality.

Part 1

1.

Goals and goal setting

I F YOU WANT LIFE TO BE fulfilling, meaningful and authentic, you have to identify your own personal goals. The moment you say to yourself, 'I'm prepared to commit to my personal goals,' you'll unleash a powerful process that sharpens the mind and directs the focus. Soon you will raise your game and start living life with a sense of certainty and conviction. This is when you will begin to create an ideal life for yourself.

In this chapter I show you how to both identify and formulate your goals. By doing so you will be embracing a winning strategy that every successful individual has mastered. You will start to harness providence and attract the things you desire into your life. Once you're clear about what it is you want, you'll see how many opportunities are available to you every day.

Successful goal setting is all about aiming for something in life that you really want. If you spend time thinking about what's really important to you and why you want to achieve it, you're on the right track to successful goal setting.

You could be forgiven for thinking: hey, this isn't me – it's only the lucky few who have this magical ability to attract what they desire into their lives. But think for a moment: haven't you already had the experience of surprising yourself in the past? Haven't you unconsciously set yourself goals and followed them through?

Perhaps you did this when you studied for an exam or landed a well-paid job, or even saved up for a really special outfit that flattered your figure. And don't forget those goals that are more wide-reaching than material gain and bring personal growth. Perhaps you put an end to a feud by letting bygones be bygones; showed self-worth and made it to the gym for an action-packed workout; were there for a friend in need; found the right words to comfort a family member or partner, or felt a significant connection with a spiritual, religious or personal belief. I'm referring to the times when you have been impressed by your ingenuity, resourcefulness and tenacity – when you've tapped into your inner core full of strength, compassion, aspirations and unique skills.

What you need before you begin

Having a diary is an essential tool for organising your week, and I suggest you equip yourself with an A4 diary/journal that allocates a full page for each day. You need to schedule in all your usual commitments and have room in the diary for the little goals you will be working on every day. You will also need an A4 lever-arch file for the various forms and information I will be asking you to gather. A selection of coloured pens/pencils and highlighter pens will also be very useful.

Now it's time to unlock your full potential and take your life to the next level.

The power of the written word

So much is possible when you tease out your goals and get them down on paper: you make them real. Identifying and writing down your goals gives you a life map, so that instead of ambling along the road with no idea where you're going, you suddenly have directions to your destination. I always ask my clients to write down their goals and refer to them every day. Without fail, they find it makes an enormous difference.

Is it really possible that a simple pen and paper exercise can transform your life? The answer is *yes*. Here's a typical reaction from a client called John: 'As soon as I got my goals down on paper they felt real and I stopped wasting time trying to validate them in my mind. I look at them every day and it's almost like having an inner voice to guide me.'

So what's the trick? Why is this simple exercise so effective? It's because when you go through the process of getting your desires down on paper you are sending instructions to your subconscious. Positive instructions then begin to produce positive results – it's that simple. I tell my clients, 'The difference between a dream and a goal is the written word.'

There is compelling research to back up the effectiveness of this exercise. It started over fifty years ago with a student survey in a prestigious American university.

In 1953, Yale University approached all their final year students and interviewed them as part of an extensive piece of market research. Questions put to the students ranged from their opinion on staff, academic facilities, courses and food, to life in general. One of the questions was: 'Do you have goals?' Just 10 per cent of the students replied that they did. The following question was: 'If you have goals, do you have them written down?' Of the 10 per cent, just under half said that they did.

Exactly twenty years later Yale University carried out a worldwide search to find their former students and discover how their lives had developed. It was a tough assignment – many of the former students were halfway around the world – but the effort was worthwhile, because when they were tracked down the Yale professors made an astounding discovery: the people who had both formulated and written down their goals had lives that were dramatically different from their cohort. Not only was their standing in the community higher, but also their health, general well-being and personal relationships were dramatically better than those of the rest. The really staggering statistic that came out of the study was that – in terms of financial success – the students who had written down their goals were worth more than the rest of the students put together!

Had I not persuaded my client Mike to write down his goals, he could have missed out on an amazing transformation. Here is his story.

Case study

Mike, aged forty-two and recently separated, came to see me dressed in a big, shapeless T-shirt, unflattering tracksuit bottoms and dirty trainers – this is what I call camouflage clothing. He was unshaven, his hair was untidy and – most telling of all – his nails were bitten to the quick. Mike was becoming depressed with his increasing weight and was desperate to improve his levels of self-worth. Of course, he was aware that his appearance was dishevelled, but said, 'I'll do something about it when I'm feeling better about myself.' I pointed out that he was in for a long wait, because the only way to feel better was by taking some immediate action, starting with his appearance.

I helped Mike to work towards a series of small goals that I asked him to write down. The goals were aimed at getting him fit and in shape, boosting his confidence and dramatically changing his appearance.

A week later Mike's scruffy locks were cropped into a sharp, sleek style that took five years off him. Feeling happier about his new appearance, Mike stopped biting his nails and threw out virtually his entire wardrobe. He then embarked on a healthy eating regime and exercise programme. He enlisted the help of friends: some went jogging with him, while others provided tips on clothes and what to wear. One friend even wrote a list of all the qualities they admired in Mike to help boost his self-esteem.

A month later and a stone lighter, Mike was wearing a Paul Smith shirt and an ultra-cool pair of Levi's. It was a revelation. With his newly discovered confidence and easy manner, he had transformed into one sexy-looking guy. I was thrilled when he told me, 'I hardly recognise myself. I can't stop looking in the mirror and smiling.'

As well as getting Mike to write down his goals, it was crucial to show him how to word them in a positive way. It was important to confirm what he was aiming for rather than compound or highlight the problem: it would have made no sense for Mike to set himself the goal 'lose weight'. He was already depressed about that, and reminding himself of the problem only sapped his motivation. It needed just a subtle change of wording to kick-start his motivation. I suggested he write down: 'I want to get my body in great shape.' By doing this, Mike's focus shifted from the problem to the solution and – because his mind was now focusing on a positive – he automatically started to think about what he needed to do to move towards his goal.

Supporting yourself

Effective goal setting requires you to apply what I call self-supporting techniques. These techniques allow you to create the right conditions for peak performance, and to demonstrate that you have the necessary willpower, motivation and mindset of a winner. I'm sure you're already an expert in helping others to achieve peak performance. For example, has there ever been a time in your life when you saw someone struggling to accomplish something? Maybe in a work situation a new recruit had been employed to answer the phone. They had a really good phone manner, but were unfamiliar with the switchboard system. You stepped in and showed them the basic mechanics of how it worked. As a result of your directions, the new recruit was able to demonstrate just how good they were. Without your valuable input, they could have appeared incompetent and not up to the job.

The point is that you didn't doubt their ability. You provided support. It's a wonderful trait to be one of life's enablers – by that I mean somebody who helps others achieve their goals. However, many of life's enablers doubt their own ability to achieve personal goals. They give themselves an unfair disadvantage, and I'll explain how. When you experience a problem or setback, does that indicate you are somehow lacking? No, of course not – but if you really want to support yourself you have to treat yourself with the same nurturing attitude that you give to others. Just spend a few minutes thinking about the contribution you have made to those you love, care about and see potential in.

Imagine doing just a fraction of that for yourself. Imagine identifying your own goals and striving towards them with heart-felt conviction, secure in the knowledge that any perceived personal shortcoming today is no more than tomorrow's history lesson. Keep reminding yourself that when you have a desire to learn, the lesson soon follows. The ability to bring out the potential in others confirms that you have the ability to bring out your own potential. All you have to do is invest that ability in yourself.

Let's get you thinking about where you are in life right now, why you need to focus on every area of your life and how to set positive goals.

The seven steps

Before I begin a one-to-one session with a client, I get them to complete a simple exercise using a life chart that indicates how they're feeling. The life chart covers seven major areas of life:

- Health

- Finances

- Work/career

- Family/extended family

- Friends/social life

- Personal relationships

- Spiritual/religious life

Use all the above seven steps when you set goals, because they encourage you to pay attention to every area of your life. This surprises a lot of my clients, who say, 'Eileen, what is this? I'm just interested in improving my finances. I didn't come to talk about friends, family or health.' The truth is that without balance in your life nothing will work. It's not enough to have a fulfilling career if your personal relationship is being neglected, or a fit, healthy body if you aren't enjoying the company of friends.

I speak with personal conviction when I say this, because I've made the mistake of putting my work and career before everything else. I paid a horrific price for it. Eight years ago I was living the high-flying business life in the centre of London. I was working very hard and my business was doing spectacularly well. This allowed me to live in a sumptuous apartment and get invited to lots of celebrity parties – for each one of which I chose a new piece of designer clothing. The company was winning business awards I had once only dreamed of.

From the outside I looked as though I had everything, but I was running on empty. I was skipping meals, working long hours and never making time to see my family. I had a boyfriend, but I wasn't putting in the time to keep the relationship going. I remember my final words to him as a partner. I said, 'The business is more important to me than our relationship.'

Now I look back and cringe. I realise how foolish I was to ignore the feelings of others, and, to be perfectly honest, my own feelings, because what I was doing wasn't making me happy.

Things came to a painful conclusion when a nagging back pain I'd had for months became so bad that I booked myself in for an MRI scan. The consultant studied the results with an amazed look on his face. He said, 'Do you have a very high pain threshold?' I told him to give me a strong painkiller because I had a meeting in half an hour. He just shook his head, saying, 'You aren't going anywhere. You have two slipped discs compressing your sciatic nerve. I'm amazed you can even stand up.'

I certainly wasn't upright for much longer. The pain became excruciating to the point where I had to lie on the floor for six weeks. It took spinal surgery to get me back on my feet – and some serious self-reflection to get my life back on track.

Whoops, I hadn't meant that to happen. So you see this goal-setting process brings results, but at a very high price when you only concentrate on one area of your life. I want the best for you in every aspect of your life – and I don't want you to make the mistakes I did. So I'm going to take you through each of the seven steps.

Health

Conditioning the mind and body allows you to get the best from them and use them to their full potential. By incorporating some minor changes in your lifestyle, major results can be achieved. A fitter, healthier body, along with mental stamina and a stress-free mind, is the optimum state to be in. Your goals should aim at getting you fit for life.

Finances

Take control of your finances, and establish your true value. Have clear goals that encourage you to work to a monthly budget and save for the future with, for example, pension schemes and life insurance. Create a healthy attitude to money, and avoid sleepless nights and patterns of overspending. Assess how much money is enough.

Work/career

Assess your current job – why you do what you do. Are you getting what you really need? What do you really want to do? When you set goals in this area you can develop new skills, deal with work-related problems, make the sort of career advancements you always wanted and get the most from your work.

Family/extended family

Try to get on with the people that fate, not friendship, chose for you. Maintain harmonious family relationships, and deal with conflict and unresolved issues. Know how to set boundaries and respect the boundaries of other family members. Live by your own values, but show consideration for other people.

Friends/social life

Recognise the value of forging strong friendships and having the support of individuals you can trust. Remind yourself what you expect from friends and what you are willing to contribute. Make time for a lively and active social life that offers variety, fun, stimulation and the opportunity to expand both your mind and body. Experience the exciting challenge of trying something new, and broadening your view, cultural appreciation and social awareness.

Personal relationships

What do you need from your personal relationships? Use goals to create the relationships you really want, move you out of the wrong relationships and bring the right relationships into your life. Develop the courage to ask for what you want, believe you deserve it and acquire the essential skills to maintain it.

Spiritual/religious life

Spiritual and religious beliefs are central to many people's value systems. They remind you that as well as having physical and emotional needs, you have spiritual needs, too. Setting goals in this area keeps you in touch with what some call a higher purpose. I like to define it as a very personal conviction that is not determined by materialistic gain. Rewards come in the form of the feeling that you have enriched your soul.

Remember that the key to having a balanced life comes from getting into the habit of setting goals in each of the seven areas. Each is equally important and relates to a significant personal need. The more needs you satisfy, the more fulfilling and complete your life will feel. You are not a one-dimensional person, who is limited in either capabilities or needs. You have depth, and living life to the full is the best choice you can make.

Exercise

THE LIFE CHART

Now I'd like you to complete the life chart, which should take no more than two minutes. This is base camp: the point from which you will set out. Give yourself a score for each of the areas that reflects how you feel right now. If you couldn't be happier, circle nine or ten. If you're really miserable and discontented, give yourself a one.

	Low								*High*	
Health	1	2	3	4	5	6	7	8	9	10
Finances	1	2	3	4	5	6	7	8	9	10
Work/career	1	2	3	4	5	6	7	8	9	10
Family/extended family	1	2	3	4	5	6	7	8	9	10
Friends/social life	1	2	3	4	5	6	7	8	9	10
Personal relationships	1	2	3	4	5	6	7	8	9	10
Spiritual/religious life	1	2	3	4	5	6	7	8	9	10

As you work through the rest of this book I will be referring you back to your original score and assessing how much progress you are making.

Assessing your current position

Where you are in life is a result of the values and aims you've been focusing on so far. What I'd like you to do now is to look at the seven life areas I gave you and think about the sorts of goals you have. I'll give you examples of how to phrase a goal in a positive way.

Health
- Get fit.
- Eat a healthy diet.
- Visit a nutritionist.
- Improve muscle tone and flexibility.

Finances
- Keep an accurate record of monthly income and outgoings.
- Save 10 per cent of my salary.
- Pay all bills by direct debit.
- Start a pension plan.

Work/career
- Get a promotion.
- Build better relationships with clients and colleagues.
- Increase my skill base.
- Improve my performance.

Family/extended family
- Talk to my family more.
- Be there for my family.
- Be a loving and understanding parent.
- Improve my relationship with the in-laws.

Friends/social life
- Catch up with old friends.
- Go to the cinema/art gallery/museum.
- Be a good listener.
- Plan more social get-togethers.

Personal relationships
- Have a loving and supportive relationship.
- Spend more quality time with my partner.
- Communicate better with my partner.
- Find the relationship I really want and deserve.

Spiritual/religious life

- Increase my knowledge and understanding of other spiritual teachings.
- Get in touch with my higher self.
- Become involved in charity work.
- Meditate on a daily basis.

Goal-setting guide

To help you set goals I have reproduced the form I use in my coaching sessions. You will find the form at the back of the book (see page 244). I suggest you photocopy it to A4 size and keep it in your lever-arch file.

Sample form

I have completed a sample form for your reference. You are not limited to setting only three goals for each area. However, it makes sense to prioritise the goals you want to work on right now; when you have achieved them, you can move on to the next set of goals.

HEALTH

Goals

1. *Get my body in shape.*

2. *Improve muscle tone and flexibility.*

3. *Eat a healthy diet.*

Personal strengths

1. *I am committed to achieving my goals.*

2. *I have the ability to put my mind to something and stick with it.*

3. *I am willing to try a new approach and not repeat old habits.*

Immediate challenges/blocks/problems

1. *I am depressed about how much I weigh.*

2. *I am too embarrassed about my body to go to a gym.*

3. *I am constantly comfort eating.*

Development skills

1. *I need to focus on what I want to achieve rather than the problem.*

2. *I will find out about exercises I can do at home so as not to use my embarrassment as an excuse to do nothing.*

3. *I will learn about nutritional food and prepare a week's shopping list so that I don't shop randomly and buy unhealthy foods.*

Achievements

1. *Get my body in shape.*

2. *Improve muscle tone and flexibility.*

3. *Eat a healthy diet.*

Here are some additional guidelines for filling in your forms.

Goals

Make them positive, what you want to achieve not what you're trying to eliminate. A goal is a gain, so think about the body you want to gain – not the pounds you want to lose. Think of faith and belief being enlightening, not confusing; work as pure enjoyment, not toil; money as abundant, not in short supply; love as heart filling, not heartbreaking; family as giving, not taking, and friends as kindred spirits you selectively choose.

Personal strengths

This is where you concentrate on your strengths, not your weaknesses. Identify what you have to offer, the qualities you are proud of, which may include being honest, loyal, hard-working, loving and forgiving, and having a great sense of humour. Don't be modest; rake in all the compliments you've had over the years, even the ones you might have previously dismissed. Ensure that the strengths you list are applicable to the life section you are filling in. For example, in work/career, being responsible and reliable would be a more appropriate strength than being in control of your money, which would be more at home in the finances section.

Immediate challenges/blocks/problems

This is where you get the negative things out. Focus on a problem that directly affects you – don't list problems that blame or involve other people. By doing so, you'll be able to see what part you play in finding a solution. It's the difference between stating, 'My work is boring' and 'I find my work boring.' The first example will keep you blocked because the emphasis is on the problem being with the job, not how it affects you and how you feel about it, but the second example will prompt you to do something about it, like finding out what sort of work you would find fulfilling. In the personal relationship section, writing: 'My previous partners have all been unfaithful to me' won't give you the same kick-start as writing: 'My problem is being attracted to people who treat me badly.' Bringing the problem back to you is not about self-blame and recrimination, but rather about taking control of the situation and understanding that you have the power to change it.

Development skills

This is any area you can develop and improve. Listing these is a great way to focus on how you can move forward. A goal to write a short story and have it published could be realised by taking a creative writing course; a goal to improve on your interview technique may require you to sign up to an adult education course in presentation skills. If stress is affecting your concentration, relaxation methods could be the answer. A useful question to ask yourself in this section is: 'What do I need to improve on in order to achieve my goal?'

Achievements

List achievements you are proud of. Begin with the big ones and keep going. Think about what you have achieved today. I want you to really pay attention to this. In fact, this is so important that I won't settle for less than five achievements you have made today. I have no doubt that during the course of your day you have found the solution to a problem, put a smile on someone's face and also demonstrated patience and consideration. I could go on, but I'm sure you can fill in the gaps.

Breaking down your big goals into little goals

The sample form identifies big goals, i.e. get my body in shape, improve muscle tone and flexibility, and eat a healthy diet. What I'm going to do now is take the first goal – get my body in shape – and show you how to break it down into a series of small goals that can be incorporated in your daily diary.

If you read through the sample form, you can see from the list of immediate challenges and blocks that the individual in question is overweight. However, as I pointed out in the previous guidelines, you must avoid using the goal section to identify the problem. So let's focus on getting a body in shape and the sort of little goals you can add to your daily diary.

Monday

8.30 a.m.   Run up and down stairs for five minutes.

9.30 a.m.   Drink two glasses of water.

10.30 a.m.   Practise some muscle- toning exercises sitting at my desk at work (e.g. holding in stomach muscles for a count of ten seconds and releasing).

11.30 a.m.	Substitute coffee and biscuits for glass of water and piece of fruit.
12.30 p.m.	Use stairs at work instead of lift.
1.30 p.m.	Buy healthy sandwich for lunch instead of sausages and chips in local café. Have a brisk walk around park before eating lunch.

Are you starting to get the idea? Going by the above diary entries, you would be six hours into your day and would have made six positive changes that would take you towards achieving the goal – get my body in shape. I'm sure you will agree when I say that all the above little goals are completely doable. By putting little goals in your diary you will stay focused on making small, positive adjustments to your daily routine. And just imagine how you will feel at the end of the day if you are able to tick off twelve little goals that you have achieved.

I'm going to be reinforcing this message constantly, and as you work with me through this book it will soon begin to feel like second nature to you.

Getting comfortable with success

You need to get comfortable with the idea of success. Look for role models that inspire you, the sort of person you could see yourself associating with, who has characteristics you admire and want to replicate. They can be from any walk of life; they might be famous, a friend or a family member. They could even be someone you met on a train. It doesn't matter. The important point is that you see their appealing traits. There is a positive association with their happiness, success and well-being. They have found a means of achieving their goal that you can relate to.

Here's something to watch out for: it's a common misconception to believe that the only people who achieve goals are ruthless, ambitious individuals who would walk over anyone to get what they want; who see success as blazing the trail on a route that is littered with casualties. This belief then – unsurprisingly – holds them back. Yes, there are people who are entirely selfish and self-serving. However, the vast majority of successful people are the complete opposite. In their pursuit of success they have enriched their own life and the lives of many others.

So – if you have it – put aside the idea that success means an all-or-nothing approach. Determination and passion can be 100 per cent, and you can still have time for all the other important aspects that occupy your life. No area needs to be neglected; the price of success is your commitment, not the sacrifices you have to make along the way. This is something my client Sonia discovered when I introduced her to the 10 per cent method.

Case study

Sonia, aged thirty-six, had given up work to stay at home and look after her two young children. When the youngest started school Sonia felt that it was time to go back to work, but she wasn't interested in returning to her previous job as a physiotherapist. She was also adamant that she didn't want to work nine to five in an office all day. She told me, 'I feel like a stupid housewife, incapable of making any decision unless it involves the kids or what's for dinner this evening.'

We spent the session discussing Sonia's life and what goals she had achieved. She was happily married, had two healthy children and ran an immaculate home. Added to this she was highly organised, and could whip up a soufflé with ease and invent imaginative and stimulating games for her children. Sonia had a wide circle of friends who valued her opinion and advice. During our half-hour session it soon became clear to both Sonia and myself that she was far from stupid and extremely capable of making major decisions. It also became apparent that she was achieving most of the things that really mattered to her.

I asked Sonia to spend just a few minutes every day thinking about the type of work that would appeal to her, and suggested she browse through the recruitment section in the newspaper. A week later Sonia said, 'I find myself drawn to sales positions, especially ones that involve selling anything to do with the home, like kitchens or bathrooms. To be honest, I've always liked the idea of working in sales.' With just a little direction and a practical suggestion, Sonia was able to own up to her real work interest. That interest subsequently became a goal that she began to work towards. Day by day she gathered information on sales positions. Within a few weeks she had a vision of herself driving to appointments in her company car, meeting up with clients and closing a sale. Six weeks after our initial coaching session, Sonia had an interview with a well-known kitchen company and was offered a job. She received training, and then got the job and a company car. Due to her fantastic ability to clinch a deal, she is now the sales team leader.

Sonia loves her job and the rest of her life. Finding a career she loves didn't involve upheaval or sacrifices – just a few minutes every day thinking about the sort of work that she would enjoy.

Action proves commitment

A sense of excitement comes from the feeling you get when you think about what your life could be like. Hold on to that feeling and keep the momentum going by taking action. Small actions fuel your confidence, so never underestimate them. Do something today that confirms your commitment to a goal. Pick up the phone, get some information, say no to something you don't want, ask for something you do want. Donate to a charity, or perhaps be totally honest with someone you have been holding back on. Do something and do it now!

When John F. Kennedy pledged in 1961 that America would land a man on the moon 'before the decade was out', he was clear about his objective. The process of achieving that objective took money, risk, intelligence, research, planning and obviously total commitment. Objectives can take a long time, even a lifetime, but to achieve a massive objective you have to achieve a lot of little goals. Every action you take and every little goal you achieve contributes to the bigger picture of your life. Creating the life you

want is a big objective, but I can't emphasise
a small effort on a daily basis and never losi
is what will produce the big results.

2

SUMMARY

- Goals come from a deep-rooted desire to create the quality of life you really want.
- Make sure the goals you set are ones you really want.
- Commit to your goals and unleash the power of providence.
- You already possess the power to make a difference.
- Write down your goals.
- Goals must be worded in a positive way – about something you want to get in life, not something you want to get rid of.
- Support yourself.
- Assess your current position and keep monitoring how it improves.
- Use the seven steps to set goals for every area of your life.
- Get comfortable with success.
- Once you have set a big goal, you can add little goals to your daily diary.
- Show your commitment by taking a small action today.
- Creating the life you really want is a big objective and requires you to achieve little goals.

Changing for the better

YOU ARE NOW READING Chapter 2, and that shows you've committed to me as a coach; you've committed to the Little Goals, Big Results approach, and most importantly you've committed to yourself.

Now I just want to check that you have done the exercises in the previous chapter. I know it's easy to skim, and I do understand if you've done that, but I want you to get the best out of this book. And if you want this book to change your life, then – trust me – you *have* to do the exercises. If you've skimmed, go back and do the exercises right away.

Welcome to the next stage of the Little Goals, Big Results programme. Let's start with some good news. As you now know, identifying goals is a fantastic exercise. When I cover goals with clients I see their eyes widen and their voices fill with enthusiasm, and frequently they seem to grow in stature. It is electric. But now the bad news. All too often after they've taken this leap forward they take a step backwards. The goals they've worked hard to discover start to feel beyond their grasp, and inevitably that first flush of excitement and enthusiasm diminishes.

What causes this? It's a little gremlin called the Limiting Personal Identity (LPI). Perhaps you've already started to hear a little LPI voice nagging in your head, saying that the goals you've found are for somebody with more time, or more talent, or somebody younger than you. Once that voice gets your attention it will *really* go to town, perhaps telling you that you lack the energy, or the confidence, or what's the point anyway when things always turn out the same? The initial boost that fired you up will start to fade. Here's my message: it's not enough just to have goals – you must also become the person who can achieve them. This involves change, and it's what we are going to work on in this chapter. Your LPI voice has to be confronted, because it's the voice that keeps telling you: 'can't change – won't change'.

The secret to getting a different result in life is to do things in a different way. However, that's not as simple as it sounds, because most of the time when people think they are doing something differently, they are actually doing it in the same way or a very similar way. I'll explain that with a simple analogy.

Let's say that every time you mow your lawn it ends up too short and with a few bald patches in it. So you try mowing it from a different angle – you start at the top of the garden instead of the bottom. Then you try going from side to side. But regardless of how you approach the problem the results are the same, the reason being that you didn't adjust the lawnmower and change it to the right blade setting.

I shared this story with my client Peter. He was adamant that he had tried everything under the sun to resolve the problem with his girlfriend and their disagreement over a holiday location. Peter had gone ahead and booked an action-packed sporting holiday. His girlfriend wanted a quiet beach with total relaxation. What had Peter done to resolve the problem? He had reverted to what I call the good cop, bad cop approach.

One minute Peter was being really nice to his girlfriend in an attempt to sweet-talk her and cajole her into agreeing on the holiday. The next minute he was ranting and raving and accusing her of being totally selfish. I'm sure you're familiar with Peter's approach, because most of us have used it. Of course, the bottom line is that you might modify your tone and delivery, but the message is the same – you're not budging or making any changes.

Luckily, Peter got the point of my lawnmower story and booked a holiday location that offered the best of both worlds.

I want to ensure that you don't experience 'same old, same old', where you feel as though you are doing things differently but getting the same results. First I'm going to introduce you to a powerful mantra for change. Then I'll show you how to make effective changes by altering the way you think – how to stop the LPI voice and how lasting change and development is possible with the 10 per cent approach.

Let's start with what I call my mantra – a statement that's simple but radical: you can develop, you can grow and you can change. Redefine yourself and you'll be amazed just how easy it is to reinvent yourself as the person you really should be. In his book *Awaken the Giant Within*, Anthony Robbins says, 'Whatever you call identity is simply what you've decided to identify with.'

I want you to stop now and read that last paragraph and Anthony Robbins' quote again. It might be the most amazing thing you hear today. Indeed, it might be the most amazing thing you hear this week or indeed in your lifetime – and I bet it's already driving your LPI mad!

I meet many people who *want* to change, but then they'll be listening to their LPI voice and suddenly they say things like, 'Eileen, *can* people really change? You can tell me, off the record. I won't tell anyone else. It's not true, is it?' One client I had, called Mandy, said, 'Eileen, I've come to you for hard business advice, but don't give me any of that coaching nonsense about people changing, because I know that it just doesn't happen.' She went on, 'You can change a light bulb, you can change your underwear and you might even be able to change your husband, but a leopard can't change its spots and people don't change either.'

Boy, was Mandy's LPI vocal that day! I told Mandy what I've just told you, and now I'm going to say it again: 'Let's start with something really simple but radical: you can develop, you can grow and you can change.' Now that's the third time you've read that. Before I say it for a fourth time, I'll tell you about a client called Vicky. I saw Vicky transform before my eyes in the space of an afternoon – and this change was lasting and real. As a coach I live for moments like this.

Case study

When Vicky came to me she was forty-five and a successful producer for a national radio show. She was having problems – she felt – because she found it impossible to switch off from her job. She illustrated this point for me in the first five minutes of our session when she refused – point blank – to turn off her mobile phone during our meeting.

Well, I thought, this is going to be an interesting session – let's follow it and see where it goes. After twenty minutes I heard the shrill ring of her phone. Vicky picked it up and flipped the mouthpiece. As she listened her top lip curled into a snarl, and then she barked, 'Are you a complete idiot? If you haven't got a suitable guest confirmed for the show by the time I get back to the office Heads Will Roll.' Then she flipped her phone closed, turned to me, smiled sweetly and said, 'So what were we taking about?'

Vicky was showing all the signs of being an out-and-out bully – not an attractive feature – so I asked her to describe a bully to me. Without hesitation, she said, 'I'm an expert on that subject, because I have personal experience of being bullied.' I nodded while she told me that as a child her father had habitually accused her of being weak-willed and pathetic. Then, when she went to school, she was (unsurprisingly) very shy, and therefore a natural target for the playground bullies who made her school days a misery. Despite this Vicky made it to university, and by that time she had decided that she wasn't going to let herself be bullied any more.

She said, 'I aimed at being assertive, having an opinion and standing my ground. But I sometimes felt misunderstood. No one appreciated how hard I worked, the decisions I made and how tough it was staying ahead in a cut-throat industry.'

Vicky was no fool. She was able to answer my questions about the difference between being assertive and being aggressive, having an opinion without negating the opinion of others and how to inspire staff without intimidating them.

Then, after forty minutes of talking, Vicky suddenly lowered her head and started to cry, and seconds later broke down in a flood of tears. In a moment of epiphany, Vicky had realised that she *had* indeed discovered the way to stop being bullied, and that was by becoming a bully herself. It was a painful revelation for her, but – to her great credit – her willingness to be self-aware allowed her to change, develop and grow.

Over the next month Vicky set a very high standard for the person she wanted to be. This involved making a list of her highest values and committing to them every day. By doing this she was able to remain decisive (an essential requirement of her job), but by learning to listen to staff and be supportive she was also able to create a harmonious team. As a result, the staff was much happier and so was Vicky, because by appreciating others the positive feedback she craved was soon returned. Vicky later told me, 'I came to you feeling angry, confused and misunderstood. I left feeling like myself.'

So now, for the fourth and final time, I'll say let's start with something simple but radical: you can develop, you can grow and you can change.

Growing pains

Now I've told you how you *can* change, I feel it's only fair to warn you that change is often not an easy process; indeed, it can be painful. However, think about this for a moment: a lot of times in our lives the things we strive for demand effort, and personal growth is no exception.

Why should change hurt? Well, as we grow up most of us develop patterns of behaviour and identities that both provide comfort and avoid pain. We do it all the time without realising it. Here's an example to illustrate what I mean.

I have a friend called Nick who tells me he just can't resist a particular brand of chocolate biscuit. He says, 'I'm a chocoholic.

If Hobnobs are in the house I eat the whole packet!' Eating a whole packet of these biscuits is part of Nick's identity, part of what makes him who he is.

Eating gives Nick pleasure and comfort. To justify it he identifies himself as the sort of man who can't say no (the voice of his LPI). He may know it's wrong and it may even make him sick (I mean, a whole packet!), but it has become a pattern that he is caught in, and when he tries to break out of it he will find he's trapped between a rock (the biscuits that will make him fat, but give him pleasure) and a hard place (his LPI telling him he has no willpower). So if Nick wants to break the pattern he's going to go through a bit of pain.

To make the process easier, the first thing Nick has to do is stop identifying himself as a chocoholic and someone who can't say no. If Nick continues thinking about himself in the same way, not only will he experience unnecessary pain, but also there is a good chance that he will set himself up to fail. It's very difficult to break a habit – especially one you enjoy – when your thought process is constantly ingraining the habit into your personality.

Changing the way you think about yourself takes effort, and because you are required to do something you aren't familiar with it's easy to slip back to your old way of thinking and behaving. A very natural reaction is to feel comfortable with what's familiar even when it's not favoured.

When an alcoholic falls off the wagon they don't think they can't wait until they hit the ground. They know the end result of their addiction has serious consequences. While you may not have the problem of an addiction you are hooked on, your behaviour patterns, even the negative ones, like avoiding emotional pain, putting yourself down, reacting angrily to confrontation or being a workaholic, can become part of your identity.

Case study

Eve Cameron was something of a workaholic when she was editor at *She* magazine. It was a prestigious job and she loved it, but as time passed she found that the high-pressured day full of deadlines, schedules and work-related evening functions meant squeezing the rest of her life into a few hours in the evenings and at weekends.

When Eve decided to leave her job, she was surprised at how much pain it caused. She says, 'I experienced a bit of an identity crisis. I kept explaining to new people I met who I had once been!' But Eve's pain was short-lived as her identity adapted to fit her new circumstances. 'Gradually,' she says, 'I settled into my new life and I'd wake up every morning excited about what the day could bring.' As an added bonus Eve lost weight, which she puts down to being in control of her life.

Let me finish this section by telling you a story about my own personal fight with my LPI.

Case study

When I tell friends that I used to be shy and fearful they laugh, but it's true. The little girl at St Frances RC primary school who grew up to take the Gucci Business Award and gave speeches all over the world was once too shy to say 'Boo' to a goose.

I remember being at school and even before the class started I was terrified that the teacher would ask me a question. Even when I knew the answer, the idea of having to speak in public mortified me. My mouth would become dry and my stomach would feel as though I had dropped twenty floors in a lift. Of course, back then I didn't realise I was letting my LPI rule my life. But it was: my shy and fearful persona made me feel trapped and racked with self-doubt.

Fifteen years after leaving school I was running my own company. My PR and one of the great mentors in my life, Fiona Harrold (who is now a hugely successful coach and author), insisted I attend a talk given by PR guru Lynn Franks. The talk was part of a series of business seminars sponsored by the London *Evening Standard*. Lynn gave an enjoyable and inspirational talk, and Fiona had a surprise in store for me. She had booked *me* in to give a talk.

I agreed, but immediately began to regret my decision. A voice from the past – my old LPI – started making mischief. Write my own speech and then deliver it to a paying audience! What on earth am I thinking of? They'll all be asking for a refund. What do I know about business? There will be experts there with degrees in business and qualifications I haven't even heard of. By the end of the day, I had talked myself from a state of apprehension to one of utter terror. I seriously needed to get a grip, and if I was going to give a talk I really had to talk myself up – and that's exactly what I did.

Over and over again I kept repeating to myself: 'You can do this, Eileen.' I reminded myself of all I had achieved so far. There had been a time when faced with a room full of strangers I would have stood motionless with my back pressed to a wall hoping to go unnoticed. But I kept pushing myself to approach strangers and make the first introduction. Eventually, it felt like second nature and I overcame my fear. Lots of other things now came easy to me because I had pushed myself, like complaining in a restaurant about unacceptable food or service, putting my own ideas forward in a business meeting, trusting my instinct and judgement, standing my ground on a point of principle and appearing on live TV. I also reminded myself that my company was very successful, and even though I had no qualifications in business, I certainly had a business story to tell. It was my personal story, and it contained valuable information that you won't find in a business reference book. I was qualified to speak about business; not only had I gained experience – I was achieving results.

On the day of my talk I felt confident and positive. I had taken the time to prepare my speech and rehearse it. My parents and sister were sitting in the front row, and a sea of faces was waiting for me to talk – and talk I did. I gave it my all. The feedback from the audience was wonderful, and I received a letter from Anthony Hilton, managing director of the *Evening Standard*, saying: 'We had an overwhelmingly favourable response to the seminar you conducted,' and one from the organiser saying: 'Thank you very much for a superb presentation.' I was elated. At that stage in my life I knew I had the ability to triumph over one of my greatest fears.

Shaking off my old identity meant creating a new one and changing the way I thought, acted and behaved. The more I focused on the person I wanted to be, the more my true identity was revealed. It's a wonderful feeling, and one I want you to experience first hand.

The transformation is achieved by taking those small steps I keep mentioning. It might begin by having a mirror as your audience, so you can check your body language and posture; using a tape recorder, so that you can hear when your voice trails off or sounds nervous; giving a presentation on any subject that interests you to trusted friends or family members. Small, manageable goals are an excellent way to build up your confidence and take you to the next level. Every time you achieve a goal, you acquire a new skill that can be used again.

I liken my experience to having a whole new wardrobe at my disposal. To have the life I really wanted meant changing as a person, throwing out stuff that no longer fitted or reflected the image I was after. Haven't we all had the experience of going shopping and trying on lots of different outfits, and then gazing at the reflection in the mirror and wondering whether it was us? Well, perhaps it is you; the only way to find out is to step out wearing something different. Present yourself in a new way and see how it feels.

Preparing to take the first step

There are numerous opportunities in life to change direction, your decisions, the house you live in, your job, partner, what you eat, how much you exercise and what you do in your free time. But when was the last time you contemplated changing your identity? The idea can seem unnerving, because there are probably things about you that you like and don't want to change. That's great: you can retain all the good stuff and simply let go of any of the negative stuff that stops you being the very best you can be. Why settle for being second best or average when you can be exceptional?

I want you to join me wholeheartedly in this journey of change. You owe it to yourself to be the best you can be; to get in touch with what's really important, significant and meaningful to your life.

Let's recap on what you have to do in order to change. Firstly, you have to believe it is possible and that's why it's great to use the mantra I suggested, and better still to make it personal – I *can* develop, I *can* grow and I *can* change. Repeating this helps to reprogramme the subconscious mind and root out any misgivings to the contrary.

Listing achievements reaffirms what you have accomplished so far and provides you with something that will convince you that it's possible – evidence. The human mind loves to have evidence to confirm a concept or theory, and it's definitely not so keen on working on blind faith alone. Imagine how difficult it would have been for me to convince myself that I could handle public speaking if I hadn't reminded myself of socially challenging situations I had overcome and how I had learned to express an opinion in public.

Provide as much evidence as possible: list all the things you have done that demonstrate you have made changes, learned new skills, overcome a fear, and changed your attitude and approach. Was there a time when you saw yourself as a person who would never be able to learn to drive, know your way around a computer, have a stable and fulfilling relationship, drop a dress size or have the stamina to complete circuit training?

Talk yourself up. You are in total control of that LPI voice in your head, so turn up the volume and start giving yourself some credit. If you find this difficult, write down what it is you are feeling and what you fear most. It looks a lot less scary on paper, and it can also help you to identify what small, manageable steps you can begin with before trying to jump the final hurdle. For example, if you want to ask someone out for a date but are afraid of rejection, perhaps you'll need to get comfortable with having an easy conversation with that person. Try finding out their likes and dislikes, what makes them laugh or what sort of films they like. Prove to yourself that you're good company and it will be a lot easier to believe that you'll be a good date.

Now it's time to review the seven life areas:

- Health

- Finances

- Work/career

- Family/extended family

- Friends/social life

- Personal relationships

- Spiritual/religious life

Ask yourself this essential question for each area: do I need to change the way I think about myself to achieve the goals I have set? For example, if you want to get fit, do you think of yourself as someone who loves exercise and eating healthily? If it's your goal to resolve a problem in a personal relationship, do you think of yourself as loving and forgiving; as being an equal match, rather than a victim. If you want to downshift and swap a high-pressure job and way of life for something more balanced, do you see yourself as being adaptable and much more than your job title?

Make a 10 per cent change today and every day, and you'll soon realise that you are on your way to becoming the person who can achieve all your goals.

There's a lot for you to think about in this chapter, but the fundamental message is that how you think about yourself determines your ability to make the right changes and achieve those all-important goals. Embrace the idea of change today, and when you feel ready I'll take you to the next level.

SUMMARY

- It's not enough just to have goals; you must also become the person who can achieve them.
- You can grow, you can develop and you can change.
- Watch out for that little gremlin – Limiting Personal Identity.
- Striving for anything worthwhile requires effort, and personal growth is no exception.
- Change often hurts, even when it's for the better.
- Set small, manageable goals to increase your confidence and take you to the next level.
- List your achievements and talk yourself up.
- Make a 10 per cent change today and every day, and become the person who can achieve all your goals.

3.

Discovering the real you

YOU MAY THINK YOU know yourself quite well, but I promise you that by the end of this chapter you'll have made some amazing discoveries. I've talked about changing for the better in the previous chapter and not letting LPI get in the way. Now you are going to find out that you are a lot more than you think you are, and we'll uncover the vital qualities that bring out the real you. By identifying your values you will discover the real you and change into the person you want to be. I'll show you how to implement your values into the little goals you set for yourself every day.

Let's now get to work with a question. Who are you? You are probably drawing a blank at the moment, because that simple question is a very tough one to answer. What makes up our identity has been a bone of contention for centuries. In early childhood our identities may have been a montage of different role models, from our parents and teachers to peer groups, but somehow our unique personalities have emerged later. It's how *you* define yourself that I'm interested in – that is, your own sense of self.

After Madonna's second child, Rocco, was born, she went on stage wearing a black T-shirt with 'mother' written across the front in big, eye-catching diamanté capital letters. While she was singing she turned around. Everyone saw that on the back was written 'fucker'. What she was saying in her own inimitable way was: *this is my identity; I'm a mother but I'm also something else, so don't mess with me!*

Let's now go back to that big question: who are you? How might you answer? Would you define yourself through your relationship status or sexuality? I'm a mother, I'm a wife, I'm a single person, I'm straight, I'm gay. Or would it be through your job? I'm a doctor, I'm a secretary, I'm a manager. Maybe it would be through your likes or dislikes? I'm someone who loves my food, I'm someone who hates injustice, I'm someone who likes a glass of wine. Perhaps you'd answer by giving me an emotional state: I'm a happy person, a sad person, a thoughtful person.

The truth is that you are many things and your definition should be a vast one. So much so that I now want you to sit down with a piece of blank A4 paper and spend ten minutes defining exactly who you are. Describe yourself as fully as you can, with reference to your work, relationships and emotional states. This is not an exercise with 'right' and 'wrong' answers. Just let yourself go and write whatever comes into your head. The only thing I ask is that you are totally honest. No one is going to see this piece of paper apart from you – so be truthful to yourself.

If you don't fill the page in ten minutes, keep going back to this exercise every day until you do. The more you ask yourself *Who am I?* the more the answers will come.

This is such a valuable and illuminating exercise that I do it myself every year. I'm always surprised by what I write. Five years ago I was living in London, working hard and playing hard. Back then – while doing this exercise – I identified myself as (among other things) a businesswoman and a party animal. Now I'm living in Cornwall with my five-year-old, and I describe myself as a mother and a writer.

Don't rush ahead and keep reading – stop what you're doing, grab a piece of paper and start defining who you are, because you're in for a big surprise!

Creating an identity that allows you to succeed

Now that you've completed the exercise where you've written down the key parts of your identity – how you see yourself – we will explore the qualities you need to change.

When the actor Will Smith portrayed Mohammed Ali, he immersed himself in the character. His actions, mannerisms and behaviour changed dramatically as he found himself taking on the traits and characteristics of Ali. He even converted to Islam, Ali's chosen religion. 'I was Ali,' insists Will Smith. 'My wife and kids were living with Ali.'

This is something that many actors experience when they are preparing for a big role. Obviously, the transformation of an actor is only intended to be a temporary one, but you can see how a change of identity can produce a change in a person's belief system and then their actions.

To find the right identity, you *don't* have to take on the identity of someone else. The idea is that you become more of the person you really are and want to be.

Being positive

Every happy person I've ever met presents a strong and positive identity. Being positive is knowing what *really* matters to you. It's about living your life in line with your values, striving to give the best and looking for the best in every situation.

I have a friend called Mike who is a freelance journalist. He'd been doing a lot of work for one particular newspaper editor and things were going very well. One day he came to me and said, 'Eileen, something terrible has happened. My editor is moving to a magazine so I'm going to lose a lot of work.' Clearly, Mike was not feeling positive, or he would have seen his situation differently. I said that perhaps this was not a crisis but an opportunity, because it would open up writing for the new editor at the newspaper, and he could also keep in touch with the former editor who would – no doubt – be commissioning for the magazine. This has, indeed, proved to be the case.

Focusing on others' positive qualities

We've looked at creating an identity that allows you to succeed and at the importance of positivity, so let's keep that theme going. If you want to focus on your own positive qualities, you have to be willing to see other people's.

If you allow yourself to focus on somebody's faults, there is a danger that you will define that person in a negative way and, as a result, overlook their positive qualities. Obviously, we're all entitled to our own opinion of an individual. However, if you get in the habit of finding fault you'll become a victim of your own harsh judgement system. Soon you'll overlook your own good points and define yourself through what you think of as your weaknesses and failures.

Let's say a work colleague can't answer a question and your reaction is to think they're incompetent. Next time *you* can't answer a question you may think exactly the same thing of yourself. To give you another example, a friend may tell you they have got into debt. If your reaction is to think what a hopeless loser they are, when you face a financial crisis yourself *you* may think the same thing of yourself.

It's important to monitor how you think of and judge others because it's a good indication of where your focus is. Do you focus on the positive or the negative? If you want to know the answer, list ten people you admire in one minute flat. Go on, give it a go. If you find you are struggling, take this as a big wake-up call because you *should* be able to come up with ten people! If you can't, you need to open your mind and heart, because right now there's not enough room in it to be positive.

Focus on the positive and mentally you'll be opening the doorway to success. You'll discover what you have to do differently, what you need to learn and how you can improve. Choose a negative mindset and you'll sentence yourself to a lifetime of regrets, where you'll feel like a failure, hard done by and like someone who never gets it right.

As you can see, you really have to get this issue of positive identity right; to expand it and make it really big. It's not just a question of 'who am I?' but also one of 'who do I want to be, and what do I want to make of myself?'

Focusing on your values

We'll begin the process by uncovering your values. Positive people know what their *values* are and believe in their own value. Here is a list of common values to refresh your memory. They are not in any particular order, so use them as a reference and reminder. Add any other values to the list you can think of.

Love	Marriage	Personal growth
Happiness	Success	Achievements
Health	Freedom	Honesty
Passion	Travel	Acceptance
Integrity	Understanding	Challenges
Money	Intimacy	Kindness
Children	Friendship	Opportunities
Adventure	Humour	Security
Trust	Respect	Spirituality/beliefs
Possessions	Contribution	

Now I want you to make a list of your ten most important values – include more than ten if you feel you need to. Allow yourself ten minutes to do this. You can alter your list at any time. Values do change in accordance with both experiences and circumstances. My friend Ben used to really value his two-seater sports car. Now that he has three children he really values his tank-sized people carrier.

When you are clear about your values, you will find that the little goals you set yourself on a daily basis have a wonderful knack of incorporating your values. Here is an example of that from one of my clients, Alex, a thirty-one-year-old social worker who is married with two girls aged three and seven. Here are the bigger goals she set for herself in her diary.

Health Exercise more and pamper myself.

Finances Stick to a monthly budget.

Work/career Be more assertive at work.

Family/extended family Do more for my parents to let them know how much I appreciate all they do for me and all their help in looking after the kids.

Friends/social life See more of my friends.

Personal relationships Bring some romance back into my marriage.

Spiritual/religious life Make a contribution to my local community.

Then she broke down her big goals into little goals and incorporated her interpretation of the value love.

Monday

7.00 a.m. **HEALTH**
Goal Five minutes of deep-breathing exercises while my moisturising face mask gets to work.

Taking time for myself first thing in the morning has really helped my self-worth, and I feel that I am learning to love and appreciate myself.

8.00 a.m. **PERSONAL RELATIONSHIPS**
Goal Husband has a big presentation at work today, so slip a note into his briefcase, saying: 'Good luck, darling. Love you lots.'

Got text from hubby, saying: 'Thanks, babe. Love you.'

9.30 a.m.   **SPIRITUAL/RELIGIOUS LIFE**
Goal Telephone local Age Concern to volunteer my services for an hour on Thursday afternoon serving tea and biscuits.

Doing something for others makes me feel good and reminds me of the love I have for my faith and other people.

10.30 a.m.   **WORK/CAREER**
Goal Talk to my boss about scheduling a more realistic deadline for the report he has requested.

I love my job and the clients I work with. To fulfil my value it was important for me to let my boss know I would be doing a disservice to the family I was assessing by producing a rushed report.

11.00 a.m.   **FRIENDS/SOCIAL LIFE**
Goal Invite Sally and Pete for dinner on Saturday night.

Love my friends and spending time with them.

1.00 p.m.   **FINANCES**
Goal Spend five minutes going through my monthly budget and assessing where I can make some savings.

It's my daughter's birthday next month and she has her heart set on horse-riding lessons. Am prone to being a bit disorganised with my finances, but love treating my children, so this is a good incentive for me.

7.00 p.m.   **FAMILY/EXTENDED FAMILY**
Goal Find Teasmade on eBay for Mum and Dad.

My parents have had a Teasmade for years and the clock has recently packed in. Their model is no longer made and I'd love to surprise them with one.

I would like you to read through Alex's goals and diary entries again. Alex has a very busy schedule, and not surprisingly a very full diary. What you have read is a brief excerpt. However, Alex achieved every little goal she set for herself that day and completed all her other commitments.

Before I coached Alex, she *was* accomplishing a great deal during the course of her day, but never felt as though she was. Why was that? Well, in part it was down to something you may have got into the habit of doing, which is not taking credit for your achievements. However, there was something else wrong: Alex was not clear about her values, so much of her day felt like keeping up with commitments and dealing with random events.

Your values are screaming at you for recognition. They are part of your life, and most importantly the core of who you are. When you consciously act in line with your values, life never feels like a series of commitments or random events. When your actions are driven by your values, what you may now perceive as a task can suddenly feel like a worthy goal. For example, when Alex set the goal to spend five minutes reviewing her monthly budget, it could have felt like a task had it not been for her value of loving to treat her children, which provided a great incentive. Equally, making time to do something for her parents during a busy day could feel like a chore if it was not driven by a core value of love for her parents.

Another benefit of living life in line with your values is that you can achieve your goals while bringing out the real you and becoming the person you want to be. For example, Alex had set the goal to be more assertive at work, but she had always struggled to do this in the past because she hated upsetting people or having any sort of confrontation. To satisfy her values, it was important for Alex to feel she was acting in a loving way. Therefore when she pointed out to her boss that an unrealistic deadline would be a disservice to her clients, Alex felt, in her own words, that, 'I'm coming from a good place and there is a very good reason to put my opinion forward.'

Being positive about your values

You will have your own interpretation of a value along with what is required to meet that value. You are a positive person, so stay focused on what it is you want. Don't stop yourself from enjoying something you value by striving for perfection or allowing negative thoughts to cloud your judgement. Remember what I said earlier – none of us is perfect, so it simply makes no sense to expect relationships, health, finances, family and so on, to be perfect. I have listed some examples of values and what you have to watch out for. Remember: the best is achievable, perfection isn't.

Health Value your body and getting it in great shape.

Watch out for comparing yourself to air-brushed images.

Finances Good money management demonstrates that you are successful with your finances.

Watch out for thinking you can only be successful with money when you have more of it.

Work/career Be sure you are contributing the value you want to satisfy. If you want respect, are you giving it?

Watch out for thinking that loving your work means a problem-free workplace.

Family/extended family Think about all the things you love about your family.

Watch out for thinking that if they don't agree with you they don't love you.

Friends/social life The friends you choose are reflective of the person you are right now.

Watch out for thinking they are to blame if you don't get what you want from a friendship.

Personal relationships Appreciate all the great things about relationship.

Watch out for expecting perfection.

Spiritual/religious life Value your own beliefs and acknowledge what they add to your life.

Watch out for thinking that because you have questions you can't answer, your faith or belief is at fault.

As you work through your list of values (and relate them to each of the seven steps), make it your goal to come up with lots of positive ways in which a value can be met. Spend ten minutes every day reading your list of values and relating them to the seven steps.

Keep asking yourself the question: *what am I doing today that confirms I am living up to my values?* This is a crucial question, since it prompts you to take a planned action rather than to just react. Thus if you value family life, you'll do something to demonstrate that every day. If you value keeping your bank account in credit, you'll monitor all outgoings rather than wait for a letter from the bank about your overdraft.

If you have completed all the exercises in this chapter, well done – you've worked really hard and discovered what's really important to you. Remember the first exercise – who are you? – when I said you were in for a big surprise? Well, if there were any blanks on that A4 sheet of paper, I'm sure you can fill them in now!

With your personal values in place, the decisions you make will be appropriate to the person you are. You'll find it easier to stand firm when decisions are value based because you will be thinking about your actions and their consequences. The next time your boss asks you to work overtime, for example, you can determine what you value the most – extra money, pleasing your boss or saying 'no' because you value getting home to see your family.

...eciate why successful people have the courage
...ns and the strength to keep going even when
...ainful transitions. It's because they know what
...them – just as you do – and can make the neces-
...to accommodate change without losing sight of
who they are... what direction they want to go in.

As mentioned in Chapter 2, change requires effort. Effort takes up energy, and energy is fuelled by motivation. To feel motivated to do anything well, there has to be a good reason to do it. What better reason could there be than doing what matters most to you and satisfying your values?

SUMMARY

- You are more than you think you are.
- Your definition of yourself should be a vast one.
- To find the right identity become more of the person you really are.
- Make sure you focus on the positive.
- Identify your top ten values.
- When you set daily little goals, think about how you can incorporate your values.
- Refer to your values on a daily basis.
- Keep asking yourself: what can I do today that confirms I'm living up to my values?
- Satisfy a value in each of the seven life areas.
- Take decisive action rather than complacent reaction.
- Fuel your motivation by doing what matters most to you.

4.

Bringing out the best in you

A FRIEND OF MINE DECIDED that she had no use for a rather drab black winter coat, so she gave it to her sister. A few weeks later my friend said, 'I wish I'd never given that coat away, Eileen – you should see how my sister has transformed it. She had it dry cleaned, replaced the plain collar with a leopard print one and added some sensational black and white retro buttons. It looks amazing. I can't believe it's the same coat.'

Haven't we all done something similar to what my friend did? Haven't we looked at something and failed to see what it could be? In fact, some people do this every day when they look in the mirror. They see an image reflected back at them, and they miss seeing how much better they could look.

Transforming yourself on *every* level is profoundly powerful – a physical change definitely produces a mental one. That's why clients often leave me with more than they bargained for! Having spent several years in the beauty industry exclusively treating a host of famous faces, it would be fair to say I can't resist coaching clients on a physical makeover as well as a mental one – and my somewhat cheeky approach always pays off.

Case study

Jonathan, aged thirty-six, came to see me for some advice on a new business venture. He had an interesting story, because he'd been a conveyancing solicitor for eight years and had come to hate it. His lifestyle had become one of fast food, stress and no exercise. Then he decided to reinvent himself and his life. He left his job and began eating a healthy diet and exercising. When I opened the door to Jonathan, I was already looking at a man who had begun to change his life. Unfortunately, his image was yet to catch up! He was wearing a grey double-breasted suit that was several sizes too large for him. This was the uniform of his former life.

After establishing that Jonathan had a sense of humour, I said, 'That's a very interesting image you have, Jonathan. Do you plan on growing into those clothes, or do you just like hiding behind them?' He explained, 'This time last year I was two stone heavier than I am now. I've made some major changes, but I guess I lost sight of making any changes to my image.'

We then talked about image and personal branding for an hour. The following week Jonathan returned sporting a snugly fitting T-shirt, which showed his exercise programme had paid off. His muscles were defined and well toned. His cream-coloured jeans were close-fitting and narrow-legged, which make him look taller. Added to this, he was wearing expensive Italian loafers – without socks, which gave a quirky Continental look to his outfit. He told me, 'I was hiding behind my clothes, but the exercise you gave me on personal branding has brought me out of myself.' It did. Jonathan was in the process of starting a company as an events organiser. At our previous session he had seemed hesitant and lacking in confidence. However, with his new image he was assertive and could see himself in his new role.

Now I want to work through the Bringing Out The Best In You exercise. I have to say it's one of my personal favourites, and that it really helps you to see what changes you can make. Let's begin with the personal branding exercise and then move on to other techniques that will bring out the best in you.

Personal branding

Businesses know how important branding is. There is no mistaking a Coca-Cola bottle for one of its competitors, or the stylish ads for Absolut Vodka – I'm sure just by mentioning the name you have an image in your head. Did you know that a massive 93 per cent of all communication is non-verbal? That 55 per cent is how you look and behave, 38 per cent is how you speak and 7 per cent is what you actually say? The bottom line is: branding is vital and image sells.

However, branding is not just about products; it's about people, too. Just look at Madonna, Oprah Winfrey and Richard Branson. They have all self-consciously cultivated their own personal brands. When I think of Mr Branson I see a smiling bearded man in a hand-knitted jumper. When I think of his values I come up with words like maverick, independent and entrepreneur. This is his brand: the way he has chosen to present himself to the world, the values he's chosen to project. A great brand is irresistible, and once people know what your brand is you'll stand out from the crowd.

Here is my ABC guide to creating a great brand for yourself.

Appearance

Our association with clothes and appearance is a strong one and gives an immediate impression. How do you want to look, be perceived or described? Are you urban chic, impeccably groomed, smart casual or cutting-edge fashion? Do you look like someone who takes care of themselves or like somebody who has just rolled out of bed? Are you perceived as wacky, conformist, youthful or fashion conscious?

People make judgements about the image you present. Take control of it and make it reflective of the image you want to project. If your big goal is to smarten up your appearance and look as though you take a real pride in it, here are the sorts of little goals you can add to your diary.

Monday

8.00 a.m.   Spend an extra five to ten minutes on your personal grooming.

9.00 a.m.   Improve your posture – check that you are sitting up straight and walking with your head up, and always avoid crossing your legs or folding your arms across your body.

10.00 a.m.   Book an appointment that will improve your appearance – for a haircut, a visit to a hygienist to have your teeth cleaned or a spray/fake tan.

11.00 a.m.   Make a list of three things you are going to change about how you dress, and set a deadline to do each one, for instance to wear more colours, accessorise more with belts, scarves and hats, wear better fitting clothes, or get measured for a correctly fitting bra.

12.00 noon   Ask a friend who has good dress sense to describe your image and how they think it could be improved. If you like any of the suggestions, note down in your diary when you are going to implement them.

Behaviour

Behave like a clown, and – hey, guess what? – people will perceive you as just that. If you behave inconsistently there's a good chance people will perceive you as untrustworthy, a chameleon and – to sum up the worst scenario – a person to be avoided. Most people strive to be consistent in their behaviour because this is the most acceptable way to behave. However, consistent behaviour only produces the results you desire when it's in line with what you really believe and value.

Trying to please others is an admirable quality, but should

never be at the expense of compromising the person you want to be. Every action follows a thought, so get into the habit of thinking positively, otherwise you will follow through on negative thoughts. Don't wait until after the event – plan ahead.

Here are the sorts of little goals you can add to your diary.

8.00 a.m.	Take five minutes out to read your list of values, then list in your diary a positive action you will take each hour of the day that will allow you to satisfy a value and achieve a small goal. Let's say, for example, that you value relationships and your big goal in the workplace is to improve your relationships with work colleagues. Set little goals that demonstrate you are following through with your behaviour and actions. You could try the following little goals or use some of your own.
9.00 a.m.	Make tea/coffee for your work colleagues.
10.00 a.m.	Help a work colleague with a task they are struggling with and pass on the benefit of your knowledge/experience.
11.00 a.m.	Be more generous with compliments and acknowledge when a job is well done.
12 noon	Be more enthusiastic about what you are doing, and if those around you are pointing out negative aspects about a job in hand, do your bit to keep things upbeat.

Courtesy

Good communicators not only attract people, but opportunities as well. Let me give you an example: because I live in Cornwall, I'm often asked by tourists for directions. The amount of information I give depends on how I'm asked: the tone of voice used, if they smile and if they have good manners. This all determines whether they are *just* told how to get from A to B, or if they are also told about a lovely pub on the way or a quiet beach known only to locals.

Obviously, the content of a conversation is important, but as only 7 per cent of communication is what you say – how you say it is even more important. Communicating with politeness and respect always produces results. There is no need to be insincere or over the top. Keep it real, or better still use my acronym for good protocol. Described below are the *real* secrets of communication.

Show respect

Always demonstrate respect towards the person/people you are talking to. Think about how you can make that 10 per cent change today. Would it be respectful to ask for someone's opinion at work? Would it be respectful to consult a partner before making a decision? Would it be respectful to thank someone or return a phone call?

Make an effort

Don't be a lazy communicator. Look interested, pay attention, put people at ease, smile, and look friendly and approachable. Think about how you can make that 10 per cent change today. When your partner asks you to do something, would smiling when you agree show you are really making an effort to please? Would a simple gesture like making eye contact confirm your interest in a conversation? Would switching off your mobile phone confirm that you are giving your full attention?

Ask questions

Ask questions that are relevant to what the other person is saying and show that you are interested in them. Think about how you can make that 10 per cent change today. When a friend tells you they enjoyed a programme on TV last night, would asking them what they enjoyed about it be a better question than you immediately expressing your opinion? When someone tells you their problems, would it be better to ask a question rather than to talk about your own problems?

Listen

Really listen: absorb the information rather than just hear words and race ahead in your mind thinking about what you want to say. Think about how you can make that 10 per cent change today. Do you need to slow down and pause before you respond? Do you need further information to clarify what's being said, for example, say something like, 'Would I be right in thinking you mean...' or 'Are you saying...?' Do you need to stop jumping in with a solution or opinion and just let the other person talk?

Don't waste what you've got

There was a time when I felt disadvantaged in life because nothing seemed to come easy to me. I had no God-given talent, like a great singing voice or artistic flair. When I was sixteen I remember the results of the mock CSE biology exam being read out to the class. I knew I wouldn't be up there in the top 80 or 90 per cent, but as the results got lower and lower my heart sank. I was having palpitations when they went below 20 per cent and my name hadn't been called. The teacher read out the name of the student that got 10 per cent, and then he paused. *Maybe they lost my paper*, I thought, but no, the final student's name was called, and it was me: 'Eileen Mulligan, 3 per cent.' The room erupted into laughter. I sat with my head bowed in humiliation.

What chance was there of me succeeding in anything with such a limited ability? However, as I discovered – success is not dependent on a natural talent or flair. The vast majority of people have to work at something to get it right.

I'd like you to take a few minutes recalling your school days. Was there a real star in your class, someone who seemed to have it all: good looks and brains, popularity and talent? I bet there was. Mine was called Stephen (not his real name). Of course, I expected the class star to fly – he did so well in school. But when I bumped into him a few years after leaving school I was shocked to see how lost he looked. His hair was dull and matted, his skin greasy and his teeth yellow.

After talking to Stephen for a short time, he confessed to a serious drug addiction, and then said, 'It's OK for you, Eileen. No one expects you to do anything. You don't know what it's like having all this pressure to be something special.' He was right – no one expected much from me, but at the same time he made me really angry. How dare he waste his talent and indulge in self-pity!

As I walked away from Stephen something changed in me. A voice in my head said, 'You're not like him. You don't have his natural talents, but you have something he doesn't.' You see, I wanted to improve, be better and make the most of myself. The desire was there in me just like it is in you. I can't give you a definitive answer about what makes the difference – why some individuals with an abundance of talent never use it or develop it. Or why other individuals who have to work hard to develop their ability wake up one day and say there has to be more to life and there has to be more to me.

That feeling can be gradual, or it can engulf you overnight, but once it arrives you can never shake it off. My own change was gradual. I did a bit every day until things fell into place and felt familiar. As the saying goes, practice makes perfect. As you know by now I don't advocate perfection, but I'm a big fan of constant practice and improving your performance.

Now it's time to do the next exercise – it should take no more than fifteen minutes.

Exercise

Make a list of all the talents you have and what comes easy to you, for example:

- I'm very musical.

- I'm very sporty and athletic.

- I find it easy to learn a foreign language.

- I have a great memory for facts and dates.

When you have completed your list, write next to each item on it what you have done to use and develop a talent and what you plan to do in the future, for example 'I'm very musical and have learned how to play the piano. In the future I would like to be a piano teacher and learn how to play the guitar.'

Now make a list of the things you find difficult and don't feel you have a natural flair for, for example:

- I find it difficult to remember names and dates.

- I get a mental block when adding up figures.

- I clam up when I meet new people.

- I'm a DIY disaster.

When you have completed your list, write next to each item on it what you have done to improve your ability and what you plan to do in the future, for example 'I'm a DIY disaster. To improve my ability I have started doing some simple DIY jobs and plan to enrol in an evening course at the local college.'

The purpose of this exercise is to identify how well you are using your talents and skills, and what you are doing to bring yourself on in areas that are more challenging. Simply focusing on what comes easy isn't enough. Mastering any area that you find difficult is very rewarding and shows tremendous personal growth. Doing something well – against the odds – is the best way to convince yourself that you are indeed capable of so much more.

When something doesn't come easy, this isn't an indication that you're not cut out for it. I'm sure there are lots of things you would secretly love to be, do or try, but you are quick to dismiss them because there's a voice in your head saying, *It's not really me*. Well, it *is* you! Every time you think it isn't, you're stopping yourself from being all you can be.

If you see yourself as a sociable person who likes to have lots of friends, but in actual fact you don't go out much and haven't many friends, then there's something you're avoiding doing. This could include making the first move, appearing friendly or simply accepting invitations!

I want you to make a list of the qualities you like about your personality, along with the qualities you would like to have. Use the following exercise, inserting the qualities you have listed in place of the examples provided. Spend at least twenty minutes on this exercise.

Exercise

Example of quality I'm interesting.

How I demonstrate this I like reading and can converse on numerous subjects, I keep up to date on politics and current affairs, I'm a great storyteller, I have lots of hobbies, I never hog a conversation or talk incessantly about myself.

To improve on this quality I have set myself the following goals: read books on different subjects, try some new hobbies, visit some new places and mix with other interesting and like-minded people.

Example of quality I take responsibility for my life.

How I demonstrate this I don't blame other people, I follow through on a decision by taking action, I hold myself accountable for my thoughts, actions and behaviour.

To improve on this quality I have set myself the following goals: be constantly aware of the choices I make, be grateful for every experience and see what I can learn from it, never make excuses for not doing something and appreciate all the opportunities available to me.

This exercise encourages you to look for evidence, examine your behaviour and search for ways to take the sort of action that will move you forward. When you complete this exercise you'll feel bigger as a person because you'll have stretched yourself, and realised that there are things you need to do and lots of things you could be doing today. You will wake up tomorrow and feel like someone who has a bigger wardrobe at their disposal. You don't have to be content with wearing the same old hat when you have lots of attributes to show off.

If you see being assertive as a quality and attribute you want to develop, all you have to do is take a small action in that direction. Examples of such an action include dealing with a financial issue before it becomes pressing, allocating a time limit to a task or making a phone call you have been putting off. If you want to be more adventurous and try different things, call your local college for a prospectus on all the evening courses available (you'll be amazed at the variety on offer), go online and check out what's available at your local sports centre, and find out what's on in your area – are there any walking, cycling or book clubs?

Have a full life, not a busy life

Now is the time to build your profile and experience the difference between having a full life and a busy life. What's the difference? With a full life you can have a family life, a work life and a love life along with a cultural, recreational, social, spirituality enlightening, healthy, mentally stimulating, relaxing and adventurous life, and still have time for yourself. With a busy life you'll only feel as though you have no time for yourself and deplete your energy in just a few areas.

You have identified what's important in your life; you have direction and are making conscious choices that allow you not only to grow as a person, but also to satisfy your personal standards and values. Stay focused on making those small changes and adjustments every day, and I promise you that in a week you'll be delighted to get acquainted with the new you.

SUMMARY

- Create an irresistible brand for yourself.
- Set little goals to improve appearance, behaviour and courtesy.
- Don't waste what you've got.
- Doing something well – against the odds – is the best way to convince yourself that you are capable of so much more.
- Just because something doesn't come easy, don't think it's not for you.
- It's not enough to just think about the person you want to be – you have to be it today.
- Remember: all you have to do is make a 10 per cent change every day and keep setting those little goals.

5.

Boosting your confidence and self-esteem

THE VAST MAJORITY OF my clients have some sort of issue surrounding confidence and self-esteem; it's a big topic so this is a big chapter. All the skills we have worked on together in the first four chapters have prepared you for this. Discovering your goals, expanding your identity and uncovering your values have given you direction and focus. Combine that with self-belief and you'll be working with a formula that guarantees success.

When you observe someone who has high self-esteem and confidence, they appear to be natural and effortless. You might feel that *surely* these lucky people have been born with these qualities, that they are somehow genetically predisposed to them – that, like having blue eyes, it's more to do with nature than nurture. This is not the case. Confidence is a skill that you can learn, practise and develop. I am going to provide you with a series of exercises and techniques that – when followed through – will coach you in the art of confidence and give a mighty boost to your self-esteem.

Let's begin by looking at exactly what self-esteem and confidence are. Confidence is your sense of being able to do things efficiently and successfully; you may feel confident at work, on the football pitch or in the kitchen. Self-esteem is the opinion you have of yourself. High self-esteem equates to a high opinion, where you love yourself, and low self-esteem is a negative opinion, where you think you are not good enough or worthless. Most of us fall somewhere in the middle. Self-esteem and confidence go hand in hand and have to be nurtured simultaneously.

Now we know the definition, let's have a look at where self-esteem and confidence come from. In my experience most confident people have grown up with what I call positive coding. That might sound a bit strange, so let me explain: we are like machines in the sense that we are driven by lines of code that are instilled in us as children.

With a computer it looks like this: 1000011110011000, but with children who are encouraged positively it looks like this: *you are good at sport, you are good at exams, you get lots of things right*. Once that code is in place, your brain looks for ways to ratify it. So when you run a race at school and win, your brain goes, *oh yeah, good at sport*. The code then becomes much more concrete, and your self-esteem and confidence grow.

The brain works in exactly the same way when we are given negative code, like: *you are stupid, you always mess up, you are bad at sport*. The brain, once again, looks for ways to ratify this information. You only have to come second in the egg and spoon race to get your brain saying, *yeah, told you that you were no good at sport – you'd better give up now!* You can easily see how that would result in both low self-esteem and low confidence.

While a lot of bad programming takes place when we are children, it can also happen in adulthood. For example, when a romantic relationship ends you might feel vulnerable, rejected and unloved. You could find that you're saying to yourself, *I'm unlovable*. Before you know it, that two-word piece of code will be sabotaging your future relationships. After all, who's going to find you attractive if you yourself feel you are unlovable?

This process happened to Angela after she had a string of bad job interviews.

Case study

Angela was a talented PA with good communication skills and she was a natural filer. However, the big jobs – the jobs that should have been hers – were eluding her. 'I'm just terrible in interviews,' she said. 'I go to pieces in front of a panel.' This was Angela's bad line of code: *I'm just terrible in interviews*. No wonder she was doing so badly! I could picture Angela going into an interview, eager, qualified and smart, but with that bad line of code she had no chance, and when she received her rejection letter it just confirmed that line of code: *I'm just terrible in interviews*.

When a programme fails in a computer, the software is opened up and the line of code is changed. I helped Angela change her negative code from *I'm just terrible in interviews* to the more positive *I need to learn interview techniques*. This was a simple but very effective shift.

With the new code in place Angela set about researching interview techniques. She bought books on the subject, found useful advice on the Internet, and during our coaching sessions got in some practice role playing. A month after our first session, Angela took part in a very real and very tough job interview. She secured her dream job and she was elated.

Beginning to change your code

I'm going to take you back now to the beginning of this chapter. Remember when I said, *'High self-esteem equates with a high opinion, where you love yourself'*? Did that make you do a double-take or even flinch? It has that effect on a lot of people. Most of us are brought up to be modest and self-effacing. The idea of saying that we *love* or even *like* ourselves goes against the grain; it sounds bigheaded, egotistic and self-obsessed. But shouldn't we like who we are? And if we don't like something about ourselves, shouldn't we be doing something about it? The answers are yes, and yes again. There is a very good reason for this: you simply can't achieve your goals or live the life you desire if you believe you are not worthy, and you can't be worthy if you don't at least like yourself!

I want you to think back now to a time when you've achieved something in the past (it might have been something at school or work, or at home) and you've been slapped on the back and told, 'Well done,' and then *you've* said, 'Oh, it was nothing.' We've all done it. We have all been slightly embarrassed when we've been congratulated, when we've achieved something, but we shouldn't be – firstly, because that credit is ours and we've achieved it, and secondly, because success breeds success. If we believe we deserve the victories we win, our self-esteem and confidence will go up and we'll go on to bigger victories, but if we believe it is just luck, or we didn't really deserve it, then the victory will appear to be hollow.

Now we've looked at two really important areas of self-confidence and self-esteem. The first is that we have bad lines of code that we need to identify and change. The second is that we need to become the sort of people who like ourselves and are not afraid of praise. We are now moving towards a frame of mind that builds self-esteem and confidence.

Let's take a closer look at some of the obvious and less obvious signs that point to a problem with self-esteem and self-confidence.

The most obvious symptoms are thinking:

- I'm not likeable.

- I'm unacceptable.

- I'm fat and ugly.

- I'm inferior.

- I'm worthless.

- I'm stupid.

And also:

- Constantly needing validation from others.

- Developing self-destructive behaviour and habits like excessive drinking, smoking, drug use, under-eating/overeating, taking on too much and frequently feeling exhausted.

Less obvious symptoms are:

- Procrastination – you put off doing something because you doubt your ability or think it could be too much of a challenge.

- Being a perfectionist – thinking you have to be perfect before you are accepted.

- Being overly competitive – thinking you have to beat everyone else to feel good about yourself.

- Being self-obsessed.

- Being overly critical – you have got in the habit of thinking negatively about yourself and find fault in everything.

- Having a need to be busy and task orientated – you feel under pressure to achieve and think that by keeping busy you'll be successful.

- Putting yourself down or making self-deprecating jokes.

- Deflecting compliments – compliments embarrass you and you don't feel worthy.

- Constantly having the need to explain yourself – you are worried about what others think of you and fearful that they may get the wrong impression.

- Predicting negative outcomes.

- Talking yourself out of doing something you want to achieve.

- Lack of stability in close personal relationships.

- Close relationships always make you feel needy and insecure.

These are just some of the indications. Low self-esteem and low self-confidence manifest in a number of different ways depending on the individual they affect. Some you will find obvious, but others you will find surprising. For example, one person with low self-esteem and a negative body image may neglect their appearance and abuse their body, while another may become obsessed with their appearance and strive for perfection. Demi Moore is a good example of this. When she was asked about her enviable and much talked about body, she said her fitness regime had more to do with her low self-esteem than anything else. 'The perception was that I was so in love with my body, when in reality I was trying to overcome my insecurity.' Demi may have succeeded in creating a great body, but until her lines of code change her insecurity will remain and she will be unhappy.

To help you assess your own levels of self-esteem and confidence, I have devised the following exercise that I would like you to complete.

Exercise

Circle the scores in the lists below that truly reflect how you feel.

Likeable

0% 10% 20% 30% 40% 50% 60% 70% 80% 90% 100%

Acceptable

0% 10% 20% 30% 40% 50% 60% 70% 80% 90% 100%

Happy with my body

0% 10% 20% 30% 40% 50% 60% 70% 80% 90% 100%

Confident

0% 10% 20% 30% 40% 50% 60% 70% 80% 90% 100%

Worthy

0% 10% 20% 30% 40% 50% 60% 70% 80% 90% 100%

You may be wondering what equates to a good score. Well, that's a question that only you can answer, because you know how you feel about the figure you circle. In the section 'Happy with my body', my client Dan gave himself 50 per cent, and said, 'I was in better shape last year, Eileen. I could do with getting back in the gym instead of being out partying all the time.' On the other hand, my client Maria gave herself exactly the same score, and told me, 'I'm in my fat phase. None of my clothes fit and no way am I going out socially looking like this!'

I want you to concentrate on improving your score rather than concern yourself about having a high score or the right one. All you have to do is determine base camp – the point from which you are starting out. Most people's levels of self-esteem and confidence are only a fraction of what they could be and we are going to work towards improving yours 10 per cent at a time. Once you experience the feel-good factor of boosting your self-esteem and confidence, you'll know if there's room for improvement.

Where are the role models?

Now I'd like you to think about someone you have *great confidence* in. It might be a friend or somebody from your family, or even someone you work with. When you've decided, I want you to describe how you *feel* about them. This should take two minutes.

Did you notice that I asked for someone *you had great confidence in* and not someone *with great confidence*? I did this because it produces a much more accurate answer as to what self-confidence really is. If you haven't thought of someone yet, take two minutes and do so now because it's crucial to the next section.

Now you've thought of someone, let me explain more fully why I asked you to think about someone *you had great confidence in* and not someone *with great confidence*. When you think of a very confident person, you may well think of an extrovert: someone who is perhaps a bit loud and likes to be the centre of attention. But are these people really confident? Or are they – like Demi Moore – fuelled by their inner demons? When you think of someone that you have confidence in there is a good chance you'll be thinking of a person whose ability you have belief in and trust in, and who you believe won't let themselves down. It's these qualities that are at the heart of a genuinely self-confident person.

As you can see, some of us act in a confident manner, and appear extrovert and attention seeking. However, behaviour is not always a true reflection of how a person feels about themselves or the state of their self-esteem. It's important for you to firstly identify how being confident should make you feel – rather than behave. If you accept that confidence and being an extrovert are two different things, you will realise that confidence is something *you* can achieve.

I say that because the idea of being extrovert is too extreme for many individuals. It's also too far removed from the person they are or aspire to be. That's OK, because you can have confidence on your own terms. Some individuals are quietly confident. They seek an inner composure that would be at odds with being the life and soul of the party, taking centre stage and courting attention. Therefore identifying with the positive feelings confidence gives you – a belief in your ability, self-trust, a reassuring feeling that you can rely on yourself – will help you to see that you can achieve this desired state without compromising the essence of who you are.

Start with the small stuff and work up

In the film *Groundhog Day* Bill Murray got to relive a day over and over and over again until he changed the way he did things and got the right outcome. Now it's time to change your day and start reaffirming your self-esteem and confidence in every area of your life.

In the last section I asked you to think of someone you had great confidence in. I then asked you to write down how you felt about them. I want you to spend a minute going over those words. Next I want you to think about how – if you had those qualities – that would change your day-to-day behaviour, if you believe in your ability, trust yourself and feel secure in the knowledge that you won't let yourself down.

Spend five minutes considering the seven life areas and how your behaviour and actions could reflect your belief in your ability and trust in yourself, and give you the reassurance that you won't let yourself down.

Work through the following exercise in your diary. Fill in a percentage that reflects your position at the moment for each of the seven areas and a specific goal you have set. In the case of health, for example, if your belief in your ability to get fit is 50 per cent, put that down. Then fill in a score that reflects your levels of self-trust and how much reassurance you are giving yourself. Allow yourself no more than five minutes to do this: the quicker you put down a score, the more accurate it tends to be. For spiritual/religious life you may find it easier to refer to your belief and leave out ability.

Exercise

Health

My belief in my ability to get fit and healthy is _____ %

I trust myself in this area _____ %

I reassure myself _____ %

Work/career

My belief in my ability to find a job I love is _____ %

I trust myself in this area _____ %

I reassure myself _____ %

Now here's a ten-day challenge: you have to get those scores up, and I'll show you how. All you have to do is take a small action every day. By doing this you will trust yourself more and reassure yourself you can do it. For example, for the personal relationship area, if your belief in your ability to have a happy personal relationship is 40 per cent, then your action could be to look for evidence that will show that your ability is higher. Perhaps you have overlooked a previous happy relationship, or a time when the existing one was happy? Maybe you're able to identify previous mistakes and can list all the things you will know to do differently? You could turn your attention to finding a compromise for an existing feud. If you're reeling from a relationship that has ended, you could identify that feelings of rejection are making you feel unlovable. By talking to friends and family, you could regain confidence that you are lovable and have the ability to find a happy relationship.

What makes this exercise so effective is that you are not remaining stuck in the same position. You are working towards feeling 10 per cent better about yourself every day. With every action you take, you can monitor your progress and acknowledge the difference in how you feel. Remember what I said about confidence being a sense of efficiency in an area? Well, the more you practise, the more competent and confident you will feel.

As your scores go up for each area, refer back to the previous exercises for assessing your level of self-esteem. Guess what? Yes, you'll find you have to give yourself a higher score.

Here are some useful little goals to use in the above exercise.

Use the word *when* seven times today to talk about goals for each of the seven life areas. For example:

- **Health** When I get in shape.

- **Finances** When I save enough money for my holiday.

- **Work/career** When I find the right job.

- **Family/extended family** When I resolve the problem.

- **Friends/social life** When I throw a party.

- **Personal relationships** When I find that special person.

- **Spiritual/religious life** When I find my faith.

This is a very powerful technique for self-esteem, especially if you are in the habit of saying *if* rather than *when*. The word *when* implies this is something that *is* going to happen, whereas *if* implies that it may or may not happen.

Focusing on the other person: a great technique

The opinions you hold about yourself are deeply rooted, so rather than talk you out of them I can give you some simple alternatives to try. These are manageable and produce instant results.

Here's how one technique works in practice: let's say you are meeting someone for the first time and feel very self-conscious. You're thinking: *what can I say that's interesting? What can I say that won't make me sound like an idiot? What can I say that will make this person like me?* If you have low self-esteem you'll feel your confidence being sapped in an instant.

If, on the other hand, you take the focus off yourself and think: *How can I show this person I'm interested in them? I'd like to know more about this person. I'd like to hear what they have to say* – you'll feel a lot more relaxed because the attention is off you.

Good conversation is about making a connection, not an impression. You don't have to talk about yourself, or be witty and entertaining. Ask the other person questions, and by showing an interest in them you will make a good impression and come over as likeable.

By replacing an ineffective pattern of behaviour with an effective one, you'll have a much more relaxed conversation and counteract that self-conscious feeling. That in turn will give a boost to your self-esteem, and when you walk away you will think: *Hey, I did OK. I can do this.*

Learn how to do what works

We've all had the experience of wishing we had handled a situation differently. However, until we ask ourselves the right questions and identify a new strategy, we remain locked into old codes of behaviour. Let's look at a typical office scene that has taken place a thousand times in a hundred different cities across the world. I'm going to make you one of the characters. Remember what I said before: this is your own personal Groundhog Day!

Your work colleague Jim has a very abrupt manner and is completely tactless. Suzie in accounts confides in you and tells you how much Jim upset her that morning. You are enraged that he should have behaved so badly – *how dare he upset Suzie like that!* Then, later that day, you go to Jim all fired up and give him a piece of your mind. Jim tells you to keep your big nose out of his business. This will inevitably create an atmosphere in the office, but you don't care: you have made a stand! However, later that day, you see Jim and Suzie huddled in a corner looking very friendly and glancing over in your direction. You think: *Oh no, they've made up and now they both don't like me!*

No doubt you can see that this is a terrible scenario. There is conflict, betrayal and a lot of bad feeling – this is going to do nothing for your self-confidence! Think for a minute how *you* might handle this differently.

Now we'll go on to the second scenario.

You say to Suzie that you feel Jim has a lot to learn about people skills and go into details about how he's treated you. Then, later that day, you see Jim and Suzie huddled in a corner looking very friendly and glancing over in your direction. You think: *Oh no, I bet she's telling him everything I said about him!*

This second scene has got a little bit better because you have not directly joined the conflict by approaching Jim. However, there are still some *very* big problems, the biggest being that your self-confidence and self-esteem are taking a hammering.

Let's analyse what is happening in both scenarios: you are too eager to please, you jump in too quickly, then you feel cut when people you trusted betray your confidence. As a result of this you stop trusting others, and more importantly yourself. The result is that your confidence and self-esteem drop. For many people this is a recurring cycle. To stop this happening the first thing you have to do is be aware of it. When you feel the urge to jump in, say to yourself, 'I know this feeling; this is my signal to make a change.'

Let's go back to that scene for the third and final time and look at how it could be handled in a more positive way.

You listen to Suzie and assess the situation, but you keep your own council and inner composure, supporting her without becoming involved. Then, later that day, when you see Jim and Suzie huddled in a corner looking very friendly and glancing over in your direction, you think: *Oh, I'm pleased Jim and Suzie have resolved their problem.*

Congratulations! Navigating the minefield of office politics is a difficult skill, but you've done it! Learning to just listen is a very useful skill and will boost your levels of trust. It gives you time to consider and reflect on information, and also not to say something on the spur of the moment that you later regret. In this third scenario you've shown you know when it's appropriate to keep your own counsel or express an opinion. As a result, you have seen the best in others, and your own self-esteem and self-confidence have both grown.

Now think of an unsatisfactory situation that has recently occurred – perhaps an argument with a partner or a work confrontation that has left an atmosphere that nobody wants. Make a list of the skills you think you could further develop to get an outcome you are happy with. Your list might include:

- I'm going to spend more time listening.

- I'm inclined to lose my temper so I will take a few minutes to calm myself before acting on a situation.

- I'm inclined to trust the wrong people, but I trust myself to reserve judgement, keep my own council and allocate more time to get to know someone.

- I'm inclined to think that when someone disagrees with me they dislike me – therefore I'm going to remind myself I also have strong opinions that are not related to my opinion of a person.

By using this technique on a regular basis, you will start to change your approach and learn what works best. The more you practise it, the more competent you will become, and that will be reflected in the outcome and results you get. When you achieve good results, give yourself credit. Then spend a few minutes familiarising yourself with the sensation of having your self-esteem boosted.

Having your needs met

The desire to have your needs met is a massive one, emotionally charged with the power of a tornado. That desire is capable of wiping out every obstacle that gets in its way and also every opportunity that comes its way.

Case study

Simon, a thirty-two-year-old estate agent, arrived at my door in tears. He was in a terrible state and kept apologising for the fact that he was crying. I said to him, 'There's no need to apologise – clients do get upset, although they usually wait until the session starts.'

Simon managed to laugh at this and composed himself before telling me his dilemma. His girlfriend had accepted a six-month contract to work abroad. After she left Simon became convinced that this was a sign she didn't love him. By his own admittance, Simon was slowly destroying the relationship by constantly pressurising his girlfriend to return home. They had spoken on the telephone the previous evening, and the call had ended with Simon's girlfriend saying, 'I'm fed up with you trying to manipulate me to do what you want. I think it's time to end the relationship.' At that point she had hung up, leaving Simon an emotional wreck.

I asked Simon why he saw his girlfriend's decision to accept a lucrative contract abroad as a sign that she didn't love him, and followed this up by asking, 'Could this be an opportunity to strengthen your relationship by showing your support, and being happy for your girlfriend and her career advancement?'

Simon thought for several seconds, and said, 'Yes, it could be an opportunity if I wasn't so insecure.' Owning up to his low self-esteem was a major breakthrough for Simon. It's only when you acknowledge it that you are able to take a step back and question your behaviour.

For the next fifteen minutes, Simon continued to open up about his need for constant reassurance and about how he had tried to make his girlfriend responsible for his insecurity. Deep down he expected rejection, and he was beginning to see it was actually *his own actions* that were causing it. He had to learn how to create the right conditions to have his needs met. The first thing that had to change was his behaviour.

We spent the last 10 minutes of the session agreeing some firm ground rules that Simon was willing to commit to. He had to show an interest in his girlfriend's new job, he had to focus on keeping future phone conversations upbeat and he was not under any circumstances to ask his girlfriend to return home!

Simon found it difficult to stick to the rules for the first week, but he persevered. After two weeks he told me, 'Our phone calls and text messages are a lot warmer and more affectionate.' Within a month Simon was feeling loved again and confident that the relationship was stronger than ever.

It's only through having a high level of self-esteem that you can find an effective way to have your needs met. Without it you risk acting on insecurity, and being manipulative or too needy. You may also miss opportunities because you harbour negative thoughts about yourself that you act on by behaving in a negative way.

However, if you devise some rules and stick to them, like Simon did, any short-term *pain* is rewarded by long-term *gain*. You will experience internal conflict when you challenge and start to change opinions. Take that as a good sign – it means you are doing it properly.

Looking after your self-esteem and confidence is an ongoing task. Whenever you feel low, refer back to this chapter and go through the exercises.

SUMMARY

- Your self-esteem is based on the opinions you have about yourself – not facts.
- Self-esteem and confidence are yours to claim at any time.
- Most people have confidence in certain areas but lack it in others.
- You have to programme yourself to run on a positive line of code.
- You can have confidence on your own terms.
- Confidence is believing in your ability, trusting yourself and having a reassuring feeling that you can rely on yourself.
- Do the 10-day challenge.
- Set little goals using the word *when* to talk about goals for each of the seven life areas.
- Learn how to do what works, and come up with new strategies.
- High self-esteem allows you to effectively have your needs met.

6.

Why it has to be today

YOUR LIFE SHOULD BE fulfilling and meaningful *right now*, but with life getting more and more hectic the pressure is increasing to get more done in less time. When our lives are so cram-packed with things we *must* do or *should* do, it can feel impossible to do the things we want to do.

This chapter is about finding out what matters most to you and putting you in control of your daily life. You've already done the groundwork, by identifying your goals and values. Now I'm going to lead you to the next step: we are going to find out what's taking up your time and how to reorganise your priorities.

The most common problem I hear from my clients is, 'Eileen, I'm juggling ten jobs at once and there simply aren't enough hours in the day to get everything done!' I sometimes feel as though I'm being asked to come up with a twenty-six-hour day! Even if I could – hypothetically – this wouldn't be the answer. Most people would find that their extra two hours would soon get used up, and they would have exactly the same problems as before.

Another time 'solution' is to create an extra hour in the day by shaving time from other activities: get up twenty minutes earlier, only have thirty minutes for lunch and go to bed ten minutes later. Congratulations! You've just found a way of making your treadmill go even faster: you'll be hitting exhaustion and burnout even sooner than before!

So what *is* the answer? What will make you happy and allow you to achieve your goals? You have to *plan* your day and *prioritise* your tasks.

Think of your life like an all-you-can-eat buffet: there's masses of fantastic food on offer and your impulse is to load up your plate and eat as much as possible. However, if you do that there's a danger that you'll end up feeling ill. It's much better for you to look at the whole buffet, and *plan* what you want to eat (and what will be good for you), and only then go about selecting the food.

Planning your day acts as a simple and powerful tool, but the vast majority of us don't do it. In his book *Time Trap* Alec McKenzie states that 72 per cent of people he questioned said: 'I don't plan my day because I don't have time to plan it.' I want you to think about that for a few seconds. Are you among that 72 per cent who don't plan and, as a result, suffer from time famine?

Time management vs self-management

Case study

When Martin, a thirty-four-year-old fund manager from a top city firm, approached me he was immaculately dressed and had a professional air about him. However, after talking to him for a few minutes I could tell he was nervy. He couldn't sit still and fidgeted continuously; he spoke quickly and seemed preoccupied with other tasks that he – no doubt – had to do later that day. These were all the symptoms of a busy man running on pure adrenalin.

Martin told me that he had a hectic work schedule, saying that he left home at six in the morning and had a day jam-packed with busy meetings and tight deadlines. He finished work so late that he joked, 'I should set up a bed in my office.' Martin's long working days were no joke to his two children and wife Clare, a teacher, who felt forced to deliver this dramatic ultimatum: 'If you don't make more time for your family I'm leaving you.'

Martin had developed a simple time-management strategy that he felt would allow him to do everything. He put off all his non-work activities to the weekend. This included spending time with his wife and two children, food shopping and household chores. There was also a game of golf, seeing friends and visiting his recently widowed mother. Oh, and picking up his dry cleaning (which he usually remembered when the shop had closed), getting the car cleaned and reading the book that had sat on his bedside cabinet for several months.

The sad fact is that time is not like money. You can't borrow an hour from Monday and give it to Saturday – it simply doesn't work like that. That is what Martin was finding out. His weekend-only availability resulted in him becoming even more overloaded, and his family was dissatisfied too.

Martin realised his 'catch up with everything on the weekend strategy' wasn't working, so he asked *me* to come up with a *time-management* strategy that would allow him to do everything and please everyone. I had to break the bad news to him that I couldn't come up with the twenty-six-hour day, and I wasn't going to offer him a plan that would get his treadmill spinning even faster. I explained, 'Time management won't miraculously give you more time to control a hectic, over-scheduled day. Substitute time management for *self-management* and you will start to get a better perspective. By taking responsibility for managing yourself, you will become aware of what choices and changes you can make.'

I asked Martin to prepare a typical weekly schedule of how he spent each weekday. He was shocked to discover that after deducting sleeping time, hours spent at work and general necessities (like eating and dressing), he was only left with a couple of hours every evening. Within those hours he only had thirty minutes of free time for his wife, and ten to fifteen minutes for his children. He suddenly realised why his wife was so desperate. He said, 'I can't believe I let myself get so busy that I neglected my family life.'

In the following weeks Martin rescheduled his working days, cutting back dramatically on his hours. Of course, his boss wasn't happy at all, but Martin was steadfast. Then, over the months, the strangest thing happened: Martin's work improved and he found himself getting *more* done in *less* time. As a consequence, his bonus was unaffected and his job remained secure. The children and his wife were all delighted. She told Martin, 'It's great to have you back as part of this family again.'

Few people reading Martin's story will be fund managers, but most will be able to identify and sympathise with his situation. It's easy to get on a treadmill without thinking. Before you know it you are up to full speed and you've started to juggle a few balls and spin a few plates too! Sooner or later, however, you'll reach a point when you say, 'Enough is enough. I can't carry on like this any more.' It could happen when a friend complains that they never see you, when a child is upset because you missed their sports day, or when a doctor tells you that your blood pressure is sky high.

Now I'm about to ask you to do the same exercise that I set for Martin: I want you to record your typical week on paper. To give you an example, I've filled in a typical Monday for myself (page 82). As I work from home there is no travelling time, and I also have the flexibility of organising my working hours around my five-year-old son. Some of the activities on my list do spill over – for example, when I'm cooking my son is usually in the kitchen. Part of my fitness regime is swimming, which I often do with my son, and he likes to accompany me with the housework (generally making more mess). Like me, you may find that areas overlap and you're actually achieving a number of goals at the same time.

When you complete the section that relates to family or time with a partner, be specific about what is real quality time. Three hours crashed out in front of the television, lost in your own world, doesn't count as three hours of family time. This could actually be wasted or lost time, when you feel too exhausted to do anything else.

You may find that you have to work through your day again because you are allocating more than twenty-four hours. When life is extremely hectic, your perception of time can get skewed and not only can you think that you have more time than you actually do, but also you overestimate and underestimate the time spent on an area.

If you have the opposite problem and there are a few hours missing from your day, think about some common time robbers like interruptions, phone conversations and daily distractions. A friend of mine was surprised to discover that his quick quiz crossword took up an hour and a half. He also spent twenty minutes looking out of the window every day!

Use your diary for this exercise or the blank form at the back of this book and allow twenty minutes for it.

Overleaf is a sample chart. When you have filled in your own chart, total up the hours along each column so you have a weekly total of hours spent on working, cooking, socialising, etc. A very clear picture should now be emerging of what takes up the majority of your time.

This is a very revealing exercise, and people are both surprised and shocked at the results. Sometimes they're surprised by the time they waste, but usually they're shocked by how little time is given to the things that matter most in their lives. If that's how you feel, take a few minutes to think about how you could re-organise your week. If time indicates how you prioritise things (and there is no better indication), then my experienced guess is that you are ready to make some changes.

Changing your times

Let's look at how you can make those changes and use some useful tips and techniques.

Sleeping time

This should be a priority, and even if Margaret Thatcher could function on four hours' sleep when she was prime minister, most of us need seven to eight hours. By all means try the technique of getting up an hour earlier or going to bed an hour later if you think you are having more sleep than you need. Make sure you are allowing at least thirty minutes wind-down time before going

	Sunday	Monday	Tuesday
Sleeping		8 hours	
Work (include travel time and preparation)		7 hours	
Grooming (dressing, etc.)		40 minutes	
Health (gym) Fitness routine		1 hour	
Cooking		1 hour	
Family/partner		3 hours	
Friends/social life		20 minutes	
Housework Laundry		1 hour 10 minutes	
Errands/school run		30 minutes	
Watching television			
Time to yourself (relaxing, hobbies)		40 minutes	
Spiritual/religious life		30 minutes	
Planning time		10 minutes	
Wasted time (too tired to do anything)			

Wednesday	Thursday	Friday	Saturday

to bed. Don't wait until you get into bed to do this. Turn off the television half an hour before bed, stop reading the newspaper (especially if it's bad news you're reading) and put aside any work-related stuff. The more relaxed you are, the more restfully you'll sleep.

Work time

This usually takes up the vast majority of the day and when you add on travelling time, preparation, work taken home and stress/exhaustion time, it can be staggering. To reduce it, think about what areas you can take *immediate action* in. For example, if you are travelling to a lot of meetings, look at which ones don't need to be face to face and start handling them by phone or email. Be ruthless at sifting out the unnecessary ones and asking your-self: what is the purpose of the meeting? What do I need to achieve? Why do I have to be there in person?

Commuting can swallow up a lot of hours, and in my experi-ence any work done on the journey to and from work is not as productive as people think. That extra hour in the morning means you arrive at work to do eight more hours of the same work and find you are drained by four o'clock instead of five. Trying to squeeze in an extra hour on the way home when you're probably tired and struggling to concentrate on the same subject is also counterproductive. A more effective use of this time could be listening to a self-help tape or some relaxing music, or reading a book.

Also consider the possibility of working from home at least one day in the week. This obviously depends on the nature of your job (it wouldn't be very practical if you're an air-traffic controller), but it can be suitable in numerous occupations. When there's paperwork, reports to be written and information to be read, a day at home could be more productive than one at the office, where there are interruptions, distractions and the risk of other people loading work on to you. You can reclaim the time you would have lost commuting.

Saying no

Practise saying no at work. Your working day can expand without you noticing it as you take on more work and end up coming in earlier or going home later to complete it. Stick to a realistic day and have a list of top priorities that can be seen both by you and anyone likely to overload you with more work. By limiting your time you limit what's given and what you take on.

Practise saying no at home. Don't over-commit; you need free time for yourself. When there are a number of people in the household, it can be tempting to get distracted with their schedules. You may find yourself caught up with what the children are doing, involved in something a partner is doing or opening a bottle of wine with a flatmate. Before you know it, the hours have ticked by and you haven't done what you intended or really wanted to do. Be disciplined and tell others when you're busy, can't spare the time or have to set a time limit.

Wasted time

Several things come under this category. The periods when you are too exhausted to do anything else are clear indications to take on less. There are the times when you are interrupted or distracted: some interruptions are unavoidable, but many can be nipped in the bud. Mobile phones can be switched off, and phones in general can be left on answer machines with a polite notification to others that you are busy. Staying focused on what you're doing helps. If, for example, when you are at work you find yourself trying to balance your ruler on your pencil sharpener, or gazing mindlessly out of the window, take a five-minute break and then refocus.

Both television and computers are big culprits of wasted time. A Gallup survey found that 10 per cent of PC users spent over twenty-hour hours per week at their screens. That equates to a seventh of your life. British youngsters watch more television than youngsters in any other European country, and a stunning

86 per cent of children watch the box between four to six hours a day.

It's very easy to get sucked into a night of television. Here are some useful little goals to help you avoid watching too much television:

1. Have a television-free evening.

2. Select what you want to watch in advance.

3. Get in the habit of setting a daily time limit.

The benefits of planning your day

Now we move on to a very powerful change that you can make – planning your day. As you now know, less than 30 per cent of us plan our day, but I'm sure more people would if they only knew the benefits. You're going to write a purposeful plan that includes activities you enjoy, actions that bring you closer to achieving a goal, and decisions that are directed by your core values. You can also safeguard against time robbers because you know you can't afford to lose time.

Case study

My client Wendy, a forty-year-old single mum who worked part-time as a reflexologist, transformed her life by daily planning. She was, by her own definition, a people pleaser, and at our meeting she told me that she couldn't say no to her three sons (aged seven, eleven and fifteen), or to the constant requests for favours from friends and family. As if that wasn't enough, her treatment sessions often overran because when clients talked about their problems she couldn't bring the sessions to a close. She said, 'I hate letting anyone down and can never say no.'

Wendy completed the exercise you have just finished. Her weekly schedule clearly showed that others dictated her day. Being at their beck and call meant her life wasn't going in the direction she wanted.

Wendy was a good person and felt guilty saying no, but as I pointed out to her, 'You also have to be good to yourself.'

Over the next month, Wendy incorporated her new daily plan. She ensured that reflexology treatments stayed within the allocated time, and a rota was displayed in her kitchen delegating various tasks to her three boys and indicating her availability. There were some growing pains – mainly from her sons, who were always demanding lifts in the car or immediate attention. However, friends and family adapted quickly to hearing that Wendy would return a phone call at a more convenient time or was unable to take on a commitment.

By the end of the month, one development that both surprised and delighted Wendy was the change in her sons. 'I never expected a knock-on effect. By setting an example in managing my own time, my children are now organising their time effectively as well.'

The principle of setting an example produces results at home and at work. When Wendy used a rota to show her sons when she was available, they had to plan their time better to get lifts along with her time and attention. Similarly, when you inform colleagues in a work situation of your schedule, they get into a habit of working around it. The signal you're sending is *no*, I'm not available twenty-four seven.

Like Wendy, you may find it hard to say no, but remember what I told her: 'You have to be good to yourself.' Otherwise you'll lack the energy to remain enthusiastic and motivated about life. You also have to make time today to work towards your personal goals because there's no more time later.

How to plan your day

You are going to plan your day by using five key points.

1. You must allow time every day to plan.

2. Good planning means not over-planning your day.

3. Your daily plan should be flexible.

4. Your daily plan must include your priorities, not just the things that have to be done.

5. When you indicate tasks in order of importance, stick to that order.

Let's go through those five points in more detail.

Planning time

Select a time in the day that is best for you. This may be first thing in the morning or in the evening. It has to be a time when you won't be interrupted and don't feel tired or distracted. In no particular order, list all the things you have to do, things you feel you should do and things you want to do. From that big list (and I know it's big), highlight what has to be done that day. Now highlight what you think you should do and the things you want to do. You can't do everything, so this is when you need to prioritise the things you really feel you should do and want to do.

Good planning

Good planning means not over-planning your day, and this can be achieved by scheduling a realistic time frame for all the critical things that have to be done. Calculate how much time is left, then deduct 50 per cent of that time. I want you to do this because experience tells me that people always think they have more time than they actually do, and never allocate enough time to interruptions, emergencies or calculating how long important tasks take. Allocate any remaining time to tasks you feel you should do and ones you want to do.

If you find it difficult, keep asking yourself, *What's really important to me?* So, for example, if you feel you should be spending time with your family, but want time alone to relax, consider whether the family time would be quality time. It won't be if you're stressed and tired, but it will be if it makes you feel good about yourself and you are able to unwind in your family's company.

Be flexible

A flexible plan allows you to work it around life, rather than expecting life to work around it. Unforeseen events and emergencies occur, and other people have different priorities from you. Being flexible doesn't mean you have to abandon your plan – simply adjust it when necessary. A work task could be delayed because your computer has crashed, or a romantic dinner may be postponed because your partner is ill. Focus on other priorities from your plan and ensure they're achieved.

Include your priorities

By this I mean your personal priorities. Remember Martin, who spent most his life working and little time with his wife and children? It's amazing how we often think that what matters most to us will wait. External pressures of day-to-day life are allowed to take priority over inner contentment and purpose. However, you have to factor in your values and goals every day. They have to be included in the plan and not at the bottom of the list with things to do if you have any spare time.

Refer to your list of values to ensure they are included in your plan, and the seven life areas.

- Health

- Finances

- Work/career

- Family/extended family

- Friends/social life

- Personal relationships

- Spiritual/religious life

You can add little goals to your daily diary. Give specific time frames, for example:

Monday

8.00 a.m.   Health: twenty minutes on Stairmaster.

9.00 a.m.   Finances: ten minutes at bank paying in cheques.

10.00 a.m.   Work/career: thirty minutes clearing my in-tray.

11.00 a.m.   Family/extended family: ten minutes booking cinema tickets for weekend.

12 noon   Personal relationships: five minutes thinking about how I can communicate my feelings better to my partner.

This is your time. Claim it and plan it in a way that indicates you intend making your values and goals a priority.

Stick to the order

You know what tasks are important and require immediate attention. Get the critical items ticked off on your list first. Then, if there is a major interruption or emergency that throws your day off course, you'll at least have the satisfaction of knowing you've dealt with the most pressing areas. A popular method of categorising urgent tasks and priorities is to mark them A, B and C. Your daily plan will have a list of things to be done, and you will be able to see at a glance what areas must be dealt with in what order.

For planning to be effective, you have to stick to the order of importance you give a task, even when it means doing a difficult task first. For example, the A list could include a call to your bank in response to a letter saying that you have exceeded your overdraft and they can't honour any more cheques. You know that call has to be made, but are too tempted to make the call in the C category, which is to a friend you want to see later. That call to a friend may make you feel better for a while, especially if you unload your problem with the bank. However, the A call is the essential one and a time delay could make the problem worse, especially if a cheque bounces.

There are numerous printed day planners, palmtops and diaries to help us plan our time, and you will have your own preference. But remember: *they won't plan your day for you or manage your time*. Only you can do that, and implement the above five key points that help you balance doing all the things that need to be done, satisfying your values and achieving your goals.

SUMMARY

- Your life should be fulfilling and meaningful right now.
- You have to allocate time for the things you want to do.
- By taking responsibility for managing yourself, you become aware of what choices and changes you can make.
- You need to assess your current position and what you are doing with your time.
- Cut out unnecessary interruptions, and reduce excessive working hours and wasted time.
- Plan your day using the five essential elements.
- Set little goals with specific time frames.
- Your values and goals have to be included in your daily plan with specific time periods and actions to be taken.
- You are now ready to make time for your life.

7.

How to have a charmed life

I'M SURE YOU KNOW AT least one person who has a charmed life. Here are the signs: they seem to have an abundance of good fortune, confidence and success, and they are enthusiastic about both work *and* their relationships. If things do – very occasionally – go wrong for them, they always seem to bounce back. How do they do it? What is the trick? Perhaps they simply don't encounter the same problems as you or I do? Perhaps life has always dealt them a winning hand?

The truth is that these people have no more of a charmed life than you or I do. What makes them special is their *attitude and the advanced skills they have developed*. You have already acquired numerous skills by working through the previous chapters, and you are now *ready* to have your skills advanced to the master class level. I'm going to show you how the right attitude will make you feel blessed, and full of triumphs and achievements. By *practising the skills and techniques in this chapter, you will develop the power to create your own charmed life*.

Attitude is so important that two people can look at the same object and then describe it *completely differently*. I'm thinking, of course, about the jar of peanut butter: one person will describe it as half full, while another will describe it as half empty. In the same way two people can have the same experience, but respond to it completely differently. *Their perception of the experience and how it affects their life is determined by how they have conditioned themselves to think.*

This was demonstrated to me recently when – by sheer coincidence – I met two people within a week who had become bankrupt. Tim (as I'll refer to him) spoke of his sense of shame: he felt like a complete failure and imagined he would carry the dreadful stigma for the rest of his life. By contrast, James had a very different attitude: he saw bankruptcy as a wake-up call. He said, 'I kidded myself for years that it was OK to do a juggling act with my finances. I was in complete denial that I had a problem handling money. I know I've made mistakes, and now I'm ready to learn how to handle money properly.'

You can see the difference: Tim was using his setback to punish himself further, while James took the opportunity to confront a problem and change his attitude.

If, like Tim, you only see the negative outcome, you will stay blocked by the problem. However, if, like James, you can turn the problem around and learn from it, you will start to move *in a positive direction*.

Developing a positive belief

The life *you* are living today is determined by what you believe. Making the decision to be positive will immediately challenge any negative beliefs you harbour. For example, let's say you've made the decision to start your own business and are determined to remain positive about your chances of success. Keep your focus on that and every time a nagging doubt springs to mind (like about how many new business ventures fail), you'll find yourself seeking evidence of success stories to boost your confidence. If you really are determined to remain positive, you'll keep confronting negative thoughts and searching for ways to support positive beliefs.

Limiting beliefs *keep you imprisoned in a negative cycle* that is hard to break out of unless you consciously direct your focus on being positive. Many people don't even realise they are negative about their lives and will go as far as to tell you they are the complete opposite. My client Mary told me, 'I'm a very positive person – it's just that people like me don't get opportunities to get ahead.' She was referring to the fact that she had a working-class background, left school with a couple of exam passes and is a single mum. I explained to Mary the difference between being positive and negative by saying, 'I'm all the things you just described (working-class background, couple of exam passes and a single mum), yet I see none of them as being a disadvantage to me achieving my goals.'

Count your blessings and more will follow

When you have a positive mental attitude, you will start to see the good things both in your life and in other people. The first and most obvious change will be that you feel different. You may have the same job, partner or house, but you will start to see qualities you hadn't previously noticed. Instead of focusing on problems and all that you perceive to be wrong with your life, you will start to count your blessings. It's as if someone has removed the blinkers and suddenly everything looks much brighter. This generates the feeling of appreciation for what you have, and you feel lucky to have those things. But here's the really exciting stuff. The more you focus on all that is *positive* in your world, the more *positive* it becomes.

I'm sure you've had the experience of receiving some great news and suddenly the world looks like a very different place. People seem more helpful and smile at you, and life feels easy. Or perhaps you've fallen in love and have that heady feeling of being on cloud nine: suddenly your grumpy boss becomes more likeable and the traffic jam less annoying, and even the heaviest rainfall can't dampen your spirits!

When your mood is *positive and upbeat*, things not only look different but also are different. Why is this? It's because people respond to the signals you give off. Unconsciously, they adapt to the climate you create. If you are cool and frosty, they may well become defensive around you. If you're bright and sunny, they relax and match your mood.

Most people rely on external stimulations to lift their mood, like getting good news, falling in love or getting a pay rise – receiving a compliment can also do the trick. If, however, you stopped relying on these *exterior* events to determine how you feel, what would you be left with?

Well, the answer is a simple one – you would be left with your own interior thoughts. You have total control over your thoughts. Now I know that things often just seem to pop into our heads and it can feel as though we have no influence or control over them, but that's not true. In his book *A Complete Workout for the Mind*, Richard Lawrence says: 'You have the potential to control your own mind more than you ever dreamt was possible... exercising the mind is the key to finding success, happiness and fulfilment.'

In your day-to-day life what you focus on will affect your thoughts and behaviour. Let's say you want a new job: you are thinking about your prospects in a *positive* way so you believe you have what it takes to get the job. You believe the right job is out there for you, and you also believe there are plenty of people on hand to give you support and advice. As you can see, when you start with one positive thought others follow.

If, however, you think in a *negative* way, then you think there are no good jobs out there and even if there were, who would give one to you? You believe life is conspiring against you, that other people are born lucky or-good looking and you never stood a chance. So you can see, equally, that a negative standpoint will result in negative thoughts continually popping up.

Having a purpose

Being positive takes practice, and a great way to begin the process is by having a purpose in life. I'm going to explain this to you with the following exercise.

Exercise

I'd like you to think about how successful you have been in achieving goals in the past and circle the statement that best reflects your success or lack of it.

a. I have been very successful and have achieved the majority of my goals.

b. I have been moderately successful in achieving my goals.

c. I have had little or no success in achieving my goals.

Now here's something very interesting about the results I get from the numerous individuals I ask to complete this exercise. The majority of people that circle c) fall into the negative camp. They believe the odds are stacked against them and that life is an uphill struggle. I don't think you'll be surprised at that result, but you *will* be by this one: there is a high percentage of people who circle a) and b) yet still have a negative outlook and feel discontent with their life.

How can that be? Well, the reason is that they are still relying on outcomes and events to make them happy. Without any real purpose or faith in their lives, they find themselves chasing false hopes, dreams and ambitions. Others may perceive them as successful, but their lives are neither charmed nor blessed because they bring them no joy.

I like to give my clients this simple analogy of why you have to have a purpose before you go in pursuit of something. Think of life as building a big bonfire. You make a list for yourself of all the things that will keep your bonfire burning, and then you fill your day collecting those things. Once you have acquired them you sit down ready to enjoy the warm glow of the fire, but suddenly you discover you have no matches!

Without that vital spark to ignite your fire, all the stuff you have gathered is rendered useless. However, if you had the matches in your pocket in the first place, how you filled your day would be meaningful and you'd be able to enjoy the end result.

Without a sense of purpose that comes from a positive belief or faith, you fall into the trap of pursuing our consumer-driven culture, which needs to keep *us* greedy to keep *it* going. You constantly strive for the next upgrade: a bigger house, faster car or more possessions. However, unless you have learned how to love and appreciate the planet and those you share it with, any sense of pleasure gained from the trappings of success is fleeting.

I'm taking time to emphasise this point because clients arrive at my door and want me to show them how to achieve their goals. I can do that. I can take them through the principles of positive mental thinking, and they can get hyped up and jump around the room full of rah-rah-rah. What I *can't* do is give them a personal sense of purpose, and *without that* they can't sustain the momentum of being positive or find true satisfaction in their achievements.

What I *can* do is to advise them on techniques that help them to find purpose: allocating time for quiet reflection is a must, and meditation is a practice I strongly advise. In his book *The Tibetan Book of Living and Dying*, Sogyal Rinpoche says that meditation allows you to find the two people who have always lived with you. 'One is the ego, garrulous, demanding, hysterical, calculating; the other is the hidden spiritual being, whose still voice of wisdom you have only rarely heard or attended to. The more often you listen to this wise guide, the more easily you will be able to change your negative moods yourself.'

For many people choosing to make time for reflection allows their lives to take on a new meaning and direction. For others it can be forced on them by a serious illness or loss of a loved one that makes them rethink their lives.

As you know, spiritual/religious life is something I include in the seven life areas, and for a very good reason. Despite the decline of orthodox religion in our society, the quest for meaning in our lives continues. To embrace a positive attitude towards life, you have to embrace life itself.

What exactly do I mean by that, and what am I asking you to do? I want you to search for your personal purpose. Take time for quiet reflection, and develop your capacity to be compassionate and loving. Practise the art of thinking well of yourself and others. Keep your focus on the good things in your life. Don't ignore problems, but don't allow them to dictate your actions and behaviour. Make the decision to be one of life's optimists, and accept that nothing is permanent and all things change. Allow life to show *you* what it has to offer, and experience the feeling of having a blessed life for yourself.

Here are some useful little goals you can add to your diary:

- Spend five or ten minutes every day on quiet reflection or meditation.

- Spend five or ten minutes at the end of every day acknowledging all the good and positive things in your life. Allocate a few minutes to each of the seven life areas so that you are focusing on the positives in every aspect of your life.

- Spend five or ten minutes every day focusing on your thoughts and making them as uplifting and positive as you can. Discovering that you are in control of your thoughts and can change your mood and state of mind is very empowering.

I'm going to show you how to achieve a charmed life by taking you through the seven life areas (which you should now be very familiar with), and looking at what I call the four charms in each one. These are:

1. Having a purpose.

2. Having a positive mental attitude.

3. Having a positive belief.

4. Embracing change.

We'll be using the 10 per cent approach, and I'll be guiding you with practical examples for each area. We cover a lot in this chapter, so you might want to take just one or two of the life areas in one session.

Health

Review your form and the goals you have set for yourself.

Your purpose

Spend a few minutes thinking about the purpose of those goals. If you have a goal to get fit, list the reasons why it's important. Will the quality of your life be improved? Will you look and feel better? Will it increase your sense of well-being?

Positive attitude

Think about ways in which you can demonstrate that you are taking a positive approach. Are you making a positive association with health rather than seeing it as hard work? Are you seeing it as a treat rather than a chore?

Monitor your progress and reward achievements. If you take a brisk walk and feel breathless, remind yourself after a week of doing it that you can now do it effortlessly. Keep charting your progress: from a few lengths swimming in the pool to twenty lengths. Make a point of noticing extra flexibility, stamina and energy.

Positive belief

Ask yourself some important questions. Do I believe I can achieve my goals? Am I conditioning my mind to think like a healthy person? Am I fuelling my body for maximum performance? Is there any negative belief I am harbouring that's getting in the way of me achieving my goals? A positive belief is essential to your success, so ensure that you are constantly challenging any negativity.

Embracing change

Achieving goals always requires you to take a flexible approach, do things differently and be prepared to change old habits. When my client Amy first started doing yoga she felt awkward, clumsy and embarrassed. However, she stuck with it because she wasn't going to let negative emotions sway her into taking the easy option of giving up. A month into her programme her breathing was relaxed and her much-improved posture did wonders for her appearance.

You have to confront those feelings of being out of your comfort zone, and appreciate that initial discomfort can be a *good* sign if it shows you are making changes.

Finances

Review the goals you have set for yourself.

Your purpose

A lot of people say that their purpose is to make lots of money, but when I ask them why they want to make a lot of money, I start to hear their *real* purpose. It can range from having security, providing the best for their children or taking early retirement, to simply pursuing a hedonistic lifestyle.

Being in control of your finances – saving money and investing in your future – should be determined by your true purpose. Unless you know what it is you desire, you'll become half-hearted about your goals and lack motivation.

Positive attitude

It's easy to get caught out with this one, because you may think that only people who are reckless or irresponsible with money have the wrong attitude. Not so: if you base the majority of your decisions around money, it can literally rule your life.

Paul (not his real name) is locked in a loveless and hostile marriage. Why? Because he has too much to lose financially through a divorce. He said, 'No way am I letting a wife I dislike so much get half of the house.' So Paul has kept hold of his money, but at a very high price.

To determine your own attitude, think about any decisions you have made that involve money. They could involve buying a new house or car, or deciding to go on holiday. Perhaps you've just indulged in some retail therapy and bought something to make you feel better. You need to assess whether or not the action you decided on made you happy. Did you make a worthwhile investment, or did the decision not to spend money make you miserable?

Positive belief

Some people believe that money is the root of all evil, others that money makes the world go round. If you're good with money, you'll find it easy to believe in your ability to manage finances and to maintain them. If you have a track record of getting into debt and struggling to make ends meet, you will have to confront any negative beliefs that you have formed, for example: I'll always have a problem with money – people like me never make a lot of money, or you have to be mean-spirited or ruthless to get rich.

Embracing change

One of the things money gives you is choice. You have more choice about where you live, the car you drive and what luxuries you can afford. But what it won't buy you is *time*. With the hectic pace of our lives, more individuals are making the choice to simplify their lives: downshifting is now common, where people with well-paid jobs with long hours change for less time-consuming work and a lower salary.

Any change to your financial circumstances will involve lifestyle changes, so it's important for you to look at how flexible you are and what changes you are willing to make. When you are willing to change, you immediately find that you can make decisions based on weighing up all the pros and cons of a situation rather than panicking about financial loss.

Work/career

Review the goals you have set for yourself.

Your purpose

Your goals *have* to have a purpose. If they are no more than a *means to an end* you will *never* enjoy achieving them or feel properly motivated. So, for example, if your goal is to do a job to make you a lot of money, you may enjoy spending the money but won't have satisfaction from the work (the means). On the other hand, when you think about what *personal purpose* you have, your direction becomes focused on doing something you *enjoy*.

This may still involve a well-paid job, but one that could include your *purpose*, which might be to make a connection with others or work as part of a team. Directing a skill or talent to give others pleasure may also be your purpose. Therefore whether it's singing in a band or giving someone a massage, you are doing something to confirm your purpose.

Positive attitude

You need consistency in your attitude to other people. We all respond to the moods of others, so if you make it *your* responsibility to *set a positive mood and hold that mood*, you won't be drawn into matching someone else's negative mood. If you aim to be positive, you won't let one small setback override what has otherwise been a good day.

Positive belief

Our beliefs about work are usually formed early in life and can reflect our parents' attitudes towards work. My father was a union man and saw all bosses as power-mad tyrants. I was in my late twenties before I managed to confront and shake off his 'us and them' attitude.

Questioning your beliefs can transform your whole attitude towards work. It's useful to question the culture and values of an organisation and see if they match your own, to question why you have formed a belief and if it is accurate. Question any beliefs that are stopping you from achieving your goals.

Embracing change

Staying ahead in our fast-moving global economy necessitates upgrading, frequent training and being multi-skilled. We have a tremendous ability to adapt, grow and change. We only find it difficult when we resist or limit ourselves. Have you ever caught yourself saying, 'I'm too old. I don't like change,' or, 'I prefer doing things how I used to do them'? You need to monitor how you respond to changes in the workplace. Are you open to new things? Or are you making change hard for yourself by wanting things to stay the same?

Family/extended family

Review the goals you have set for yourself.

Purpose

For many individuals, family is one of their greatest purposes in life. You often hear people say that their family means the world to them. If that's how you feel then the purpose of the goals you have set should already be very clear to you. Supporting and strengthening that bond is a common purpose.

However, there is conflict in many families and a purpose can also be to resolve a difference or to ensure that it doesn't impact negatively on the rest of your life. Having a positive purpose will focus you on setting goals in a positive direction.

Positive attitude

My client Lawrence told me that while he had a great relationship with his wife and two children, his knuckles turned white whenever he drove to see his parents. 'I feel the tension as soon as I pull out of my drive. In the half-hour journey, I start to recall Dad's annoying habit of never looking up from the TV, and how Mum has this obsession with me needing a haircut! Sure enough, when I arrive at their home I'm in a foul mood.'

As I said before, it takes practice to sustain a positive attitude, and something as simple as not mentally recalling previous situations that annoyed you will help. When it comes to family, there may be lots of times when you have to boost your frame of mind and stop predicting disaster – and remember, family respond to our mood as much as we do theirs.

Positive belief

Our initial experience of family life forms our early beliefs. That's fine when you have a good experience, because you will have positive beliefs. The challenge is to change any negative beliefs that come from a bad experience.

My client Michael wanted to heal a rift with his father, and told me, 'I really want to believe this is possible, but my father is as difficult to deal with today as he was when I was a child, and he still makes me feel worthless.'

Michael's intentions were good: he was desperate for his father to change or for me to give him techniques that would change him. I explained to Michael that while people can be manipulated, *you* can't change *them* – only they can do that for themselves. What you can do is change yourself and stop believing that others have the power to determine your self-worth. This is one way of forming a positive belief in this area.

Embracing change

Most of us know what it's like to have parents treat us as though we're still children. Then we often go on to do the same thing with our own children. We don't always notice the changes, and it can seem as if overnight that a child becomes an adult, or a parent seems old and you notice how much they have slowed down. They start off as your carer, and you could end up caring for them.

Families encounter numerous power struggles and battles of ego and *it's all normal*. Roles change within families, and jobs and opportunities take loved ones far afield. To enjoy every aspect of family life, you have to roll with the punches and the changes.

Friends/social life

Review the goals you have set for yourself.

Purpose

Defining the purpose of the goals you have set will confirm the significance of what can become a neglected area. With friendships you should be reminding yourself of the invaluable supportive bonds that can be forged – the comfort of having someone you can confide in and share problems with. There's the feel-good factor you get from being there for a friend, knowing you get to choose these people and they get to choose you. With your social life you can satisfy and fulfil a great many, if not all, of your life purposes.

You can engage in all sorts of social activities, from eating out or watching a film, to hiring a boat for the day. You can pursue a hobby you are passionate about, enrol in an evening class or be adventurous and take up skydiving. You can use social time to take up a cause like protecting the environment, and volunteer to clean up a beach or sell memberships to the Wildlife Trust. When you ask yourself what your purpose is there's no limit to what you can do.

Positive attitude

If you're mixing with the right people and have a stimulating social life, you'll feel very positive about this area. If you've been neglecting this area and have lost touch with friends or rarely go out socially, you need to take some action.

Truckloads of friends and exciting social invitations don't suddenly arrive on your doorstep. They require effort and commitment on your part. Friendships come about when you're open to them, and the more positive your attitude the more friends you attract. You have to give people a reason to want to be around you or to have your company socially. Positive individuals are always attractive because they make the world a brighter place.

Positive belief

One of the best ways to generate a positive belief in this area is to keep company with positive, like-minded individuals. The company you keep is an accurate reflection of where you are at right now in terms of being positive. It's no good complaining about friends being selfish, always moaning and never wanting to do anything – if that's not what you're about, then jump ship and get yourself out there with the movers and shakers.

A useful discovery I made when I turned forty a few years ago was that being around young people is fantastic. I have lots of friends of my age whose company I love, but it's refreshing to mix with people who don't have children, the restraints of a mortgage or the pressures of a demanding career. We all need to be reminded about how to have fun and not take life too seriously.

Embracing change

Good friendships allow for personal growth. When your life and lifestyle change (as they do when you pursue personal development, settle down or have children), you have new priorities and demands on your time. We all feel nostalgic at times, but if you stay stuck in the past you limit your enjoyment of the present.

As your identity expands and life takes you in different directions, you need to ensure that your friends and social life reflect the person you are, and that any changes encompass the whole you. To be the person you want to be, you have to mix in the right circles and have an active and varied social life.

Personal relationships

Review the goals you have set for yourself.

Purpose

Again, your goals *must have a purpose*. Ask yourself *why* your goals are important and you will uncover the purpose. For example, if your goal is to have a happy, loving relationship, you may want that because you believe it's what will make you happy; equally, it could be that for you it's the ultimate human connection.

Positive attitude

Even the best relationships have their ups and downs. You have to ensure that you remain positive and don't let your emotions get locked into a downward spiral.

We've all had the experience of remaining upset long after an argument is over. We have then allowed that negative emotion to have an impact on the good times, thus tainting the good memories and getting in the way of enjoying new experiences. To avoid this, keep your focus on all the positive things in your relationship and keep asking yourself: what can I do to contribute to a relationship?

Positive belief

We all experience intense emotions with close personal relationships. Because of this it can be difficult to shift a negative belief that has resulted from a painful experience.

The first step is to *recognise when you are holding on to a negative belief.* Are you always recalling negative experiences with previous partners? If you are, the chances are that you not only have a negative belief, but are also reinforcing it.

The second step is to *challenge your negative belief.* Monitor what you say and how you talk about an existing relationship. Think about what your expectations are. Do you expect things to go well, or are you – because of your previous experience – continually waiting for a crisis to occur?

You wouldn't expect a fire to burn well if you kept throwing a bucket of water on it and it's the same with relationships. They are fuelled by what you believe, so choose to adopt a positive belief.

Embracing change

Change is the norm in every area of life, and relationships are no exception. Some couples grow together during the changes, while others grow apart. Heartache and being unable to move forward comes from resisting change. The bottom line is that change will occur with or without your consent, and it makes sense to be active in the process. That way you see what choices are available and what level of control you have.

Spiritual/religious life

Review the goals you have set for yourself.

Your purpose

You may already be clear about your purpose in this area, and you might even have a deep spiritual or religious conviction, but it's always useful to remind yourself what it is. If this is not an area you have yet chosen to work on, I recommend that you do so because it's much easier to have a positive outlook when you are in touch with an inner belief that promotes goodwill to yourself and others.

Positive attitude

I was brought up by my parents to be a strict Roman Catholic – my school favoured the fire and brimstone approach. As a result of this, I believed that the God-fearing Catholics were on the true path to righteousness and salvation, and that the rest, well, they were destined to damnation.

As you might imagine, the idea of playing with children down the street (who were heading straight to hell) wasn't very appealing. My childhood did not encourage a positive attitude about either my religion or other people.

Today my faith is something I'm entirely positive about, because I have a positive attitude that allows me to make a positive interpretation of it. Being positive will show in your thoughts and actions, your desire to contribute to others and to refrain from making harsh judgements, and your capacity to love and accept yourself.

Positive belief

It's usually the *interpretation* of a spiritual or religious practice that results in a negative belief rather than the practice itself.

Sometimes along the way we take things out of context to confirm a negative belief. For example, the Bible says: 'Let he who has not sinned cast the first stone.' This is a very positive statement. However, in a moment of retribution we can call on our religion to justify our mean behaviour and find ourselves thinking of the quote: 'An eye for an eye and a tooth for a tooth,' which is very negative.

We all need to self-regulate, because we are all capable of petty, selfish and negative behaviour. I find it very useful to ask myself the following question: *Am I thinking and behaving in a way that confirms a positive belief?*

Embracing change

A positive belief allows you not only to accept that all things change, but also to learn and grow from the experience. Although death is the one inevitability in life, it is a taboo subject in Western society. Yet for Tibetan Buddhists the word for body is *lu*, which means something you leave behind, like baggage. They see themselves as travellers, taking temporary refuge in this life and in this body. It's hardly surprising, then, that they are not a youth-obsessed culture, and that they don't dread old age or fear death. Any belief that encourages you to hold on to something that isn't permanent will always be limiting.

Now you need to take the four charms with you every day and act on them. Day by day you will experience the remarkable difference they bring into your life. Write them down and carry them in your purse or wallet. Look at them several times a day to keep you focused and clear about what you're aiming for.

If at any time you feel you are having difficulty in making progress in an area, refer back to this section. Mastering these techniques takes constant practice. It's hard work, but I promise that when you start to use them, your life will feel charmed.

SUMMARY

- Having a charmed life is the result of having the right attitude and skills.
- Your perception of an experience and how it affects your life is determined by how you have conditioned yourself to think.
- Making the decision to be positive will immediately challenge any negative beliefs you harbour.
- The ability to turn your life around and make things go your way comes from having the right attitude.

- With a positive attitude you will learn from setbacks and move forward. With a negative attitude you will use setbacks to punish yourself and stay blocked.
- Life delivers what you expect rather than what you deserve.
- People with a charmed life have a positive attitude combined with an unshakeable belief in what life has to offer and a willingness to embrace change.
- What you believe shapes your life.
- Your goals must originate from a deep sense of personal purpose.
- Set little goals that encourage you to focus on the positive, and count your blessings.
- Use the four charms in each of the seven life areas to achieve a charmed life.
- Mastering the four charms takes practice, so refer back to this chapter on a regular basis.

8.

Part 2

Organising your personal environment

IF YOU WANT TO MAKE changes in your life you have to create space to do it in. You need a living environment that reflects the new you and will provide you with the right surroundings to really get to work on part two of this book.

You've already created your mental space by taking on new ideas and throwing out the old ones. Now I want you to work on your physical space by organising your home. I'll be showing you how to get things in order and how to set goals that keep you organised. I don't want you to confuse having an organised home with having a super-clean show home. My mother reckons I was born with the cleaning gene and that by the age of one I could use my cot blanket to put a French polish on its wooden frame. It's true that I do love to clean and polish – however, there is plenty of room in this chapter for personal preference.

Your home is your personal space and it has to be organised. A disorganised home saps your energy: every deferred task becomes a grinding reminder of something you haven't got around to. It might be a pile of ironing, bills stuffed in a drawer or a stack of washing-up – and that's just the start. When it really goes out of control you will stop functioning properly: a forgotten bill will become a final demand and even a court order. The suit you need for an important presentation will be stuffed in a bag and will never make it to the dry cleaners, or your baby will be due for a check-up with the health visitor and you won't be able to find the check-up book you were told to put in a safe place!

It's not just 'nice' to have a tidy house; it's a vital part of your life. A well-organised home provides relaxation and harmony. It allows you to stay on top of bills, and when you want to find something you will know where it is. Soon you will find you have more hours in the day and – more importantly – your home will offer a comforting atmosphere and help to recharge your energy levels.

Defining an organised home

A home to be proud of is one that you've organised to suit *your* lifestyle. We all have our idiosyncrasies – as you know I love to clean and polish – and for some people it's making the bed the second they get up or perhaps lining up their CDs in alphabetical order. Different people have different priorities and there's plenty of room for personal preference. However, there are some basic guidelines for organising, which I'm now going to take you through.

- Your home should be safe. This means keeping it in good repair, being hygienic and considering the needs of other people. Young children and the elderly are particularly vulnerable in a neglected house.

- Your home has to meet your basic needs. It needs to provide food, warmth, shelter and safety, so you don't want to arrive home to an empty cupboard or fridge, a cold house or a leaking roof. Pay attention to the essentials, keep a well-stocked food cupboard and set the timer on the central heating.

- Your home should be comfortable and relaxing. Any extreme – being either very messy or tidy to the point of being sterile – is not conducive to creating a harmonious living space.

- Your home has to reflect the needs of those living in it. Think about what's important to you, and then make it happen. You might want a moody bachelor pad or a funky, fluffy place. Perhaps your idea of heaven is the smell of freshly baked bread, a wood-burning stove or children sitting at the kitchen table doing hand paintings.

- Your home should consist of delegated areas that suit your lifestyle. You may need a workspace, relaxation area, eating space, family room and entertaining facilities like a TV, bookshelf or drinks cabinet. There could be an area adapted for children to play in safely, a toy-free zone or an annex for an elderly relative.

- Your home has to be budgeted for. To maintain and run it smoothly, you have to live within your budget.

- House rules are a must. You need to be clear about what's acceptable in your home. You may, for example, want to make sure that the washing-up is done before you go to bed, or ask friends and family to remove their shoes before they enter the house.

- Maintaining a routine and order will keep you on top of tasks.

Adapting your home to suit your lifestyle

Your lifestyle is the first thing to take into consideration before attempting to organise your home. Cream sofas, glass coffee tables and marble floors may be great in a child-free household, but if you have children they could be inappropriate and dangerous.

I'm sure you've watched at least one of the many TV programmes on buying a home. Before the experts begin, they sit down with the prospective purchaser and discuss their needs. That's what I did for my client Melanie when she wanted to organise her home.

Case study

Thirty-four-year-old Melanie had a five-month-old baby boy and an extremely lively two-year-old son. She worked part-time from her home, which was a big Victorian house.

When Melanie came to see me she said, 'I can't believe I'm in such a mess. I'm always cleaning and tidying, yet I can never find anything. I forgot to sort out the car tax, and I'm always rushing out to the shop to buy some item of food I need. When friends came to dinner last week, it was a disaster: I was so behind that it was past ten before we started eating!'

Melanie's home looked immaculate, but if you opened any of the drawers or cupboards, you'd be buried in an avalanche of papers, grommets and widgets! She was trying to keep her home looking exactly the way it did before the children were born. The problem was that she hadn't adapted it to cater to her new lifestyle.

I complimented Melanie on her lovely house and then asked her, 'How practical is it keeping it looking like a showroom?' Melanie said, 'I know I'm overly houseproud, but if the house looked bad people would know I was struggling.' I asked, 'What's more important, organising your home to suit your family and work, or keeping up appearances?' Without hesitation Melanie conceded that her family came first, but then admitted that she'd let things get so disorganised that she didn't know where to start.

Using the 10 per cent approach, I showed Melanie how to begin by assessing her needs and those of her family. Then we used a process of setting little goals to get the results she needed.

It was a priority for Melanie to have a routine in place for her two children, and I asked her to focus on this first and to not concern herself with the housework for the first week. With the children's routine in place, Melanie could see how much time was available for other tasks and delegate time sensibly.

Trying to do everything in one go (especially with small children) is counterproductive. You can't organise paperwork, empty drawers or cupboards full of clutter, and navigate two under-fives all at the same time! By doing a little bit every day and having goals that kept her organised, Melanie was on top of the situation by the end of the month.

Now let's have a look at your home. I'm going to take you through the same process I used with Melanie, which will be equally effective for you.

Exercise

I want you to start by thinking about what you need from your home. In your diary make a list using headings. I've provided some suggestions to help you make a start.

A. I want my home to provide:

Relaxation

Comfort

A harmonious atmosphere

A safe place for the children to play

Quiet areas free from noise

A feeling of family

A safe and clean environment

An animal-friendly feel

Privacy and seclusion

A delegated work area

Once you have established what your needs and priorities are, start working towards achieving them. Under each statement you have written list a minimum of three methods of working towards your goals. I've provided two examples to help you, and the types of little goal you could set.

B. Achieving my goals:

1. It's important for me to have a clean house. To achieve this I'll:
   a Have a regular cleaning routine.

b Buy storage units to get rid of the clutter.

c Make everyone in the household aware of their responsibilities.

2. It's important for me to be organised. To achieve this I'll:

a Pin a noticeboard in the kitchen.

b Deal with maintenance and repairs immediately.

c Have a household budget.

Use your diary to ensure you are implementing your little goals. For example:

Saturday

10.00 a.m.	One hour giving house thorough clean.
11.00 a.m.	Ten minutes preparing a list of jobs and who is responsible for doing them.
12 noon	Buy storage units and noticeboard for kitchen.
1.00 p.m.	Ten minutes making a snagging list (this is a list of all those little jobs that need to be done but never actually do get done).

Don't try and take on too much at once. If every room in the house is packed to the gills like an old curiosity shop, tackle one room at a time.

Keeping your home as you want it

It's all too easy to have a cleaning blitz, congratulate yourself and then swiftly slip back into your old habits. You need to stay organised to prevent the mess from returning. Here are some good examples of methods that will keep you on track.

Define the function of a room and only allow things into it that are relevant to its function. For example, the kitchen is for the storage, preparation and eating of food. It may also house a washing machine, but it doesn't have to turn into a laundry room with piles of ironing and clean clothes. It doesn't have to be the place where everyone dumps dirty washing on the floor, and the ironing board doesn't have to be permanently erected.

To keep your kitchen organised, have a place for every-thing and a goal-orientated routine that stops mess. If, therefore, your big goal is to have an organised kitchen, there will be little goals like:

1. Always put dirty laundry in laundry basket, which is kept in the cupboard under the stairs.

2. Always put clean linen and ironing in airing cupboard.

3. Clean fridge once a week.

4. Clear work surfaces of all non-essential items every day.

5. Arrange kitchen cupboards so that items that are used fre-quently are easy to find, tins containing the same products are stacked together, and dustbins are a suitable size and not overflowing half way through the day.

A very useful little goal is to set aside ten minutes every night to check all the rooms and remove anything that doesn't need to be there.

Bear in mind that in a shared household you are not respon-sible for all the cleaning and clearing up, but you may have to take responsibility for organising these jobs. Therefore the sooner you implement your little goals to get yourself organised, the sooner you can start to delegate jobs.

Useful hints

- Adequate storage can be a problem, and if you don't have enough cupboard space you'll need storage boxes and addi-tional shelving. Large DIY chains stock inexpensive storage containers and practical shelving units.

- Most people find it hard to throw things out, but if you can put your junk to good use you'll find it easier to part with. Find out where your nearest clothes bank is, and also look for recycling centres, second-hand shops and charity shops. You could alternatively try selling your surplus items at a car boot sale or on eBay and make some money from the stuff you don't need.

- Have a cleaning routine and stick to it. Allocate how long you are going to spend on cleaning and how often, and what jobs you want to do, for example making the beds, cleaning the bathroom and kitchen, dusting the furniture, and emptying the bins and cat-litter tray. Time yourself to begin with, and don't become distracted with other jobs – if you are cleaning the bathroom, that is not the time to clear out the bathroom cabinet.

- Allocate a place for bills and important paperwork, such as TV licence reminder and insurance policy renewals. Dedicate a time every week for dealing with these. When you do this on a regular basis, it takes very little time and it doesn't feel daunting.

Exercise

WEEKLY PLAN

Below is a very manageable weekly plan. You can note it down in your diary.

Day 1

Complete exercise A (**I want my home to provide**) and exercise B (**Achieving my goals**).

Day 2

Select a room that needs organising and describe the function of that room. It could, for example, be the family and entertainment room. Now list the items that are acceptable to be in that room, which may include a TV, books, games, videos and a CD player.

Day 3

Now that you have selected a room and decided on its function, it's time to get all the stuff you'll need for the makeover. You may need to buy some storage boxes and additional shelving, and make sure you have plenty of bin bags to clear excess clutter. Recruit some help – ask a friend or family member if they would be available to help you. Decide what you are going to do with any clutter you remove – is it for the charity shop, or will it be relocated to another area of the house?

Day 4

Set aside exactly how much time you have available to clear out the room. Don't exceed that time: it's much better to do the job over a few days than to do too much in one go and be left with the memory that it's hard work – it shouldn't be.

Day 5

Arrange the room to suit its function. It's better to arrange books and videos in horizontal rows rather than stacked on top of each other. Furniture should suit the purpose of the room; there should be adequate seating and no dangerous cables or wires to trip over. You can brighten or soften the light in a room by changing the wattage of light bulbs – you may also want to add additional lighting with a lamp.

Additional suggestions

Think about who will use the room and how often, what state it's acceptable for the room to be left in and whose responsibility it will be. For example, it could be that the last person to use the room before going to bed should arrange cushions neatly, empty the waste-paper bin, replace any videos or DVDs, and turn off the lights.

Before you move on to another room, make sure you have established a routine to keep the first room in order. You may be full of enthusiasm and raring to go, but if you have children they can need a bit of time for retraining: having patience and consistency is the most practical approach.

Here's a policy I always suggest: use half the energy you have to reorganise a room in week one and keep the other half for maintaining and getting others to follow through with the routine in week two. Remember that it takes physical and mental energy to coordinate a busy household, so a little at a time is best.

Organising a flat or house share

When there is more than one person in the household, you need other people to cooperate and that can be difficult to arrange. It can be done, and once again good organisation is the key to success.

Where there are other adults and older children in the household, discuss your plans with them. Make them aware of what you want to achieve, and be enthusiastic about them having an input and making suggestions. Discuss who will be responsible for certain tasks, such as emptying the bins or washing the dishes.

Not everyone likes the idea of having a rota pinned up in the kitchen, but in my experience a rota is essential when you are establishing a new routine or keeping to an agreed one. It lets everyone know what's expected of them and so prevents misunderstandings.

We all have varying degrees of what we consider tidy and acceptable: for you, tidy may mean clean dishes, clear work surfaces and everything put away. However, for a flatmate it may mean ashtrays emptied (but not washed) and dishes washed only when they start to grow their own life form!

House rules have to be clear and specific, and if others don't comply be quick to remind them of what was agreed rather than wait until you feel angry and frustrated.

There are particular items that are always a bone of contention in house shares unless a policy is put in place. They include toilet rolls, milk and cleaning products. You could find that it's always *you* buying the washing-up liquid or toilet cleaner. Having a household budget that everyone contributes to for these items is a good idea.

My friend Linda, who shares a house with four other people, has a household budget for toilet rolls, soap, cleaning products, milk, tea and coffee. She says, 'It works really well, especially with the milk. I used to get really mad when someone in the house used up the last of my milk, but now I don't take it personally because it belongs to the household.'

Useful hints

- Sit down together and make a list of what is agreed as acceptable shared standards.

- When tasks have been jointly agreed, let every individual write down their agreed job on the rota. By putting pen to paper (literally), they are acknowledging the joint agreement and being reminded of (in their own handwriting) their responsibility to a shared household.

As I said at the beginning of this chapter: if you want to make changes in your life you have to create space to do it in. An organised home will save you time, offer a comforting atmosphere and help you recharge. You owe it to yourself to create an environment that is both conducive to and supports your commitment to achieving your goals.

SUMMARY

- If you want to make changes in your life you have to create space to do it in.
- Your home is your personal space and it has to be organised.
- A disorganised home saps your energy.

- A home to be proud of is one that you organise to suit your lifestyle.
- Follow the basic guidelines for organising your home.
- Trying to reorganise your home in one go is counterproductive.
- Keep setting little goals to help you organise your home.
- Define the function of a room and only keep things in it that are relevant to its function.
- Shared households need to have agreed rotas.
- You owe it to yourself to have a living environment that reflects the new you and supports the changes you are making.

9.

Looking and feeling great

WHEN YOU START TO GET your life in order it follows that you will want to get your body in order. That means looking your best and aiming for optimum health. By taking care of yourself you will look and feel years younger, have the energy to live life to the full and be able to focus on your goals with maximum mental clarity.

I want to do something for you that I love doing for my clients. I'm going to give you a makeover. You deserve it because you've worked hard and stuck with me through all the exercises!

I've had years of experience as a beauty therapist, massaging, scrubbing and buffing clients from all walks of life, including pop stars, TV personalities and supermodels. Along the way I learned lots of tricks of the trade, and how a healthy diet and exercise can transform the way you look. Now I'm going to share the secrets of looking and feeling great with you.

We start by addressing the issue of what makes a person attractive, the common conceptions about beauty and some of the misconceptions, too. Then we move on to what fantastic and easy techniques you can use to make you look and feel years younger. After that I show you how to get head-to-toe pampering treatments on a shoestring and achieve a body to be proud of. We finish by looking at how you can commit to self-care.

Because this is the 10 per cent approach, I'm not suggesting that you make huge overnight changes. Just go at your own pace, take one step at a time, and do what you feel comfortable with and what suits you. You'll be surprised how the right steps can transform you, and before you know it you'll have walked a very long way!

What makes someone attractive?

There are all sorts of theories. Some studies have shown that we are subconsciously attracted to people with symmetrical faces, others that we are attracted to people who look like our parents, and then there's the theory that we are attracted by scent.

I'm *sure* each theory has its own merits, but no one has ever shown *me* more about being attractive than a girl called Sharon. She showed me that attractiveness is a state of mind.

Case study

I knew Sharon back when I was nineteen and working as a waitress in a busy motorway service station in Corley. She had frizzy brown hair that sprang from the sides of her waitress hat, small eyes that disappeared when she smiled and teeth full of gaps. She wasn't conventionally good-looking, but she was always smiling and laughing, chatting to customers and at ease with everyone. People often told me I was pretty, but I was chronically shy, avoided making eye contact with the customers and often took orders while looking at my shoes.

Can you guess who got the most compliments in the customer comment book? I read them every day: 'Sharon's gorgeous, Sharon's really sexy,' and one even said 'Sharon's got a lovely bum.' The men loved her! The women liked her too; they said she was friendly and approachable. These comments – and all the tips she got – made me feel a bit envious, but more than that they totally baffled me. What had she got that I hadn't? And how come I never got any comments?

I didn't have to wait for too long for my first comment, but it wasn't what I was looking for. It said: 'Eileen walks around as if she's got a bad smell under her nose.' So there I had it: I may have been conventionally prettier than Sharon, but people perceived *her* as much more attractive.

Sharon felt attractive and that's what people perceived her as being: when you warm to a personality, even imperfections can become attractive. You begin to take in the whole essence of a person: how they move, the energy they generate and the character within them.

I'm sure you've had a similar experience – perhaps you've met up with someone for the first time and not registered that they were good-looking. However, after spending time with them, you started to notice attractive features about them. Perhaps they had green eyes that lit up when they laughed, a lopsided grin that gave character to their face or a healthy glow that radiated vitality.

You can starve yourself thin, wear the latest trendy designer clothes and Botox away your laughter lines, but if you are *not* happy and confident in yourself, you are unlikely to come across as attractive.

The perfect appearance simply doesn't exist. You are never going to be satisfied. If you are on the beauty treadmill get off it now! You will never look like Brad Pitt or Cindy Crawford, but you can – believe me – be attractive and confident, and make the most of what you've got.

How to look fantastic

Great skin

In general your skin is what people judge your age by. Start looking younger right now by drinking a glass of water (tap or bottle). Water hydrates the skin and naturally cleanses the body. Few people drink enough of it; the British Dietetic Association suggests we drink a minimum of 1.5 to 2 litres (6–8 glasses) a day. If you are drinking plenty of water your urine should be clear and practically colourless – and before you ask, no, tea and coffee do not count as water. It's got to be water, as pure as you can get your hands on.

You can look years younger by looking after your skin. Sunlight prematurely ages the skin, depleting collagen levels and causing wrinkles and pigment changes like dark patches and liver spots. To avoid this use a sun block.

If you use soap to wash your face, use a low-alkaline one. Dove's gentle pH-balanced formulation contains ¼ moisturising cream, to help retain skin's natural moisture. Better still, use a cleanser – I use Nivea. Dead skin cells build up as we get older and can be removed with an exfoliating product. Use a body moisturiser when your skin is still damp, as it will hold moisture in. Peel-off masks can be used on the face, and if you use a face flannel – which I love to use – replace it every couple of months because the slightly abrasive effect of the cotton is lost over time. Remember that skin also benefits from a nutritious diet and a good night's sleep.

If you really aren't sure what your skin type is, get some expert advice. Beauty therapists use a magnifying lamp to assess skin type and there are beauty consultants in most department stores. The service is available for men and women. There are plenty of products specifically designed for men, who have thicker, oilier skin, and there are ranges to suit different ethnic skin types.

Stress, alcohol and cigarettes all damage and age the skin. Our skin is much more forgiving when we're young and can quickly recover from bad habits, but the effects show as we get older. If you want your skin to look its best, you have to take care of it throughout your life.

Let's see how you can incorporate the above points into goals.

Exercise

If your big goals are having great skin and looking years younger, you could add the following little goals to your dairy:

Monday

8.00 a.m.   Use a body exfoliation in the shower/bath, and a body moisturiser when your skin is still damp.

8.15 a.m.   Use a gentle soap/face wash and a moisturiser that contains a sun block.

8.30 a.m.   Drink a few glasses of water.

12.30 p.m.   Visit a professional beauty therapist or department store consultant for advice on your skin type and suitable products.

9.00 p.m.   Have an early night.

Great hair

A good haircut can take years off a person and give a totally different image. Good hair products don't have to be expensive, and there are plenty to suit every hair type. Your hair, like your skin, needs protecting from the sun, and you can buy sprays and mousses that contain sun filters. Without one, hair (especially if it has been coloured) will soon look dry and dull.

On the subject of hair colours – unless you really know what you're doing – leave it to the experts. Used incorrectly, hair-colouring products can be very damaging. A good colourist will match a colour to your skin tone and blend shades to give a natural effect. We've all seen someone who has an unnatural-looking block of hair colour. It's usually an attempt to cover grey or keep the shade they had in their youth. Natural hair has different shades and skin tone changes as we age, so raven-black hair may suit you when you're twenty, but if you have it when you're forty you will look ghoulish.

Great teeth

Look after your teeth and gums. Personally, I'm not a fan of perfectly straight teeth that are the result of cosmetic dentistry. Most of us have a few misshapen molars, but we can still have a dazzling smile with clean white teeth. Teeth-bleaching and whitening treatments are widely available, and there's a good selection of whitening products available from chemists. It's important to floss your teeth. Advice on correct brushing and gum care is best sought from your dentist or hygienist.

Exercise

Get great teeth and hair with these little goals:

Tuesday

9.00 a.m. Book a hair appointment (if you are thinking of changing your hair colour, you can book an initial consultation for advice).

9.30 a.m. Check your hair products – make sure you are using the right shampoo and conditioner. You can buy products that protect your hair from sunlight.

10.00 a.m. Book an appointment with your dentist or hygienist.

11.00 a.m. Change your toothbrush regularly, and make sure you use dental floss.

Great style

In Chapter 4 we worked on personal branding and finding the right image. I want to take that a step further and make sure you're getting your image right. You need to take a close look at your wardrobe and how you present yourself.

Your clothes should reflect you as an energetic, vibrant and attractive individual. This comes from having style – which is not necessarily the latest fashion item or designer label. With style you can dress for any occasion and look good. When you see someone stylish you can't help noticing them even if they're wearing something you wouldn't choose for yourself.

Presenters Jonathan Ross and Graham Norton both have the personalities to carry outrageous and camp styles. Joan Collins is full-on Hollywood glamour, and Lulu has mastered the art of looking trendy at fifty. She can wear fashionable and youthful clothes because she's in great shape and has the vitality of a much younger person.

Developing your own style prevents you from being a fashion victim. Fashion victims wear things that are unflattering, unsuitable and overly faddish. With your own style you can build a wardrobe of timeless outfits and make alterations for changing trends or occasions. For example, a well-cut man's suit can be dressed down with a T-shirt and trendy trainers, or dressed up with a shirt, tie and smart shoes. In a similar way, a shift dress can be casual daywear or stunning eveningwear when accessorised with heels and jewellery.

Style may appear effortless, but it isn't. It takes planning along with attention to detail, and when it appears effortless it's usually because it's not overdone.

Let's start by organising your wardrobe. Start with the basics, have a good sift through you smalls and chuck out anything that's washed out, discoloured and has holes in. Next, get rid of any clothes you don't wear. If you haven't worn it for a whole year, should you really be giving it space? No!

Clothes that are out of season should be packed away – there's no point in looking at a wardrobe stuffed with thick coats and jumpers in the summer. You'll find it much quicker to choose a flattering outfit when you're not sifting through piles of clothes. Next, arrange your wardrobe in an easy-to-find way. It helps to keep long-sleeved items together and short ones separate. Display similar colours next to each other. Smart and casual shoes can be separated, and there are very useful drawer dividers available from most department stores.

Keep your clothes well laundered and smelling fresh. I'm inclined to iron towels, which I know is a bit excessive, and if you prefer not to spend too much time ironing, hang up your clothes while they are still damp so that the majority of creases will fall out.

Now it's time to think about shopping. Start small by replacing the old underwear you've thrown out. Get items that are comfortable but still make you feel attractive and sexy. A G-string prevents an unflattering knicker line (men may be interested to know that few women like a bloke in a G-string), whereas boxer shorts look sexy on men and women. If you usually buy your underwear in the same place, try shopping somewhere new.

Never think you are too old to shop in any store. Browse around and see what's in fashion, and what would and wouldn't suit you. If you identify a style that you like, you can always find a variation of it in another shop if necessary. Think about having a few different images: sporty, casual and chic or formal. Your wardrobe should be flexible and have variety.

If you don't know what suits you (or find it difficult to coordinate an outfit), choose a friend who always looks well turned out and invite them to go shopping with you. They'll be flattered that you want their opinion. Try on a variety of styles and colours rather than sticking to the same ones.

Here is a useful little goal: add some items to your wardrobe that you wouldn't usually wear.

Useful hints

- Spend a few minutes identifying the look you want to achieve. Do you want to look trendy, sexy, outrageous or chic? Perhaps you prefer traditional, timeless or classy?

- Are you dressing to suit your figure or disguise it? If you're dressing to disguise it, throw out the camouflage clothes. You'll never feel motivated by dressing down.

How to feel amazing

Pampering treatments on a shoestring

Pay attention to your grooming and treat yourself to some pampering treatments. There are numerous treatments available from colleges that train beauty therapists, aromatherapists, reflexologists and so on. In my experience, the students that are training offer very good treatments and are usually well supervised. You can get a massage or facial manicure for less than £10. An eyebrow tint and shape can transform your face, and if cellulite is a problem there are some revolutionary electrical treatments and muscle toners available.

There are colleges for homeopathy, acupuncture, Chinese medicine and every other alternative treatment. They all need clients to practise on, so get on the Internet or look in the Yellow Pages and see what the reputable colleges are in your area. Then it's just a quick phone call to see what's on offer. I often find that the treatment I get from a studious student is better than one given by someone who has been doing the job for years.

You can buy excellent inexpensive beauty and grooming products in supermarkets. Joan Collins swears by Vaseline, Nivea and any of the cheaper cold creams. I have it on very good authority that Ms Collins still looks fabulous without make-up and with her hair wrapped in a turban. She's a firm believer that being positive, happy and fulfilled keeps people younger and more vibrant. She says, 'People who look younger than they are generally feel younger than they are, and they attract people who are younger than they are – not just as lovers, but as friends, too.' Joan has a thirty-something husband – there's a gal who walks her talk.

Diet

We all know the benefits of a healthy diet. It improves the quality of your life, giving you more energy, improved skin and hair, and mental clarity.

From the billions of pounds that are spent every year in the diet industry, it's obvious that many people struggle to eat a healthy diet and control their weight. The course of action is often to make drastic changes in a short period of time. This rarely works because you need to break old habits and create new ones over a period of time.

If you're eating an unhealthy diet your taste buds need time to develop a taste for new food groups – it will be much easier to wean yourself off foods that are high in salt, fat and sugar if you do so gradually. You'll only crave them more if you suddenly withdraw them completely.

Make small, consistent changes and follow the guidelines on a healthy diet:

- Eat five portions of fruit or vegetables every day.

- Make the main part of your diet complex carbohydrates – pasta, potatoes, grain and bread.

- Limit the amount of fat you eat.

- Eat plenty of oily fish.

- Drink lots of fluid – water is the best.

- Limit the foods that are high in salt and sugar.

I'm a big fan of juicers and they're great for increasing your intake of fruit and vegetables. I have a carrot and ginger juice every morning – replace tea or coffee with a juice first thing in the morning and you'll feel the difference very quickly.

When clients find it difficult to make changes in this area, I encourage them to commit to one small change; when that becomes a habit (which usually takes a week) we move on to the next change. My client Tom had a sweet tooth and would buy several bars of chocolate on his way home from work. Every evening Tom would tell himself that he wasn't going to eat all the chocolate, but he did.

I suggested to Tom that for the following week he should buy half the amount of chocolate he usually bought. Tom found it much easier to stick to this than he thought. By week two Tom was buying one bar of chocolate every evening, and within a month he allowed himself the occasional treat. This technique worked because it was much easier for Tom to break his habit of buying chocolate than his habit of eating it.

I use a similar technique for clients doing their weekly shopping. At the time of purchase, individuals feel confident that they won't sit down and eat a whole packet of biscuits in one go, or a tub of ice cream or any other high-fat snack. However, when the trigger point comes, which can be anything from boredom and loneliness to a craving, the temptation is too much to resist. If you reduce the amount of unhealthy foods you buy gradually, you won't put the same amount of temptation in your way. As Tom found out, you'll give yourself time to break a bad habit and create a good one.

It's important to give yourself the reassurance and confidence that you can make changes. Bad habits take a long time to build up, so don't berate yourself when it takes time to change them.

Exercise

Exercise has to be something you enjoy, or you won't have the motivation to do it on a regular basis. You have to make it a positive association and find a way of exercising that feels like a treat, not a punishment. With so much emphasis on the need for discipline and willpower, it's easy to make a negative association with exercise. We tend to think of discipline and willpower being used to make us do something we either don't want to do or find difficult. However, if you think about exercise as being play time, you'll let go of limiting inhibitions and see there are lots of fun exercises.

My friend Nick, who is thirty-eight, zips around on a skateboard. Now you may think that only teenagers look cool on a skateboard, but not so. Nick looks fit, athletic and years younger than his age. He stands out from the crowd because he has the confidence to do something different and set an example.

Some exercises make you feel young at heart and mind, like bouncing around on a trampoline, or playing a game you haven't played since your school days like rounders or hopscotch. I recently bought a big inflatable splash pool for my son, and have great fun playing in it like a big kid and getting plenty of exercise in the process.

We're inclined to be too serious about exercise and have forgotten what it's like to just let go and do something our bodies enjoy. If, for example, you love dancing and meeting new people, then joining a salsa or country and western line-dancing class may give you more incentive than working up a sweat in the gym.

Don't concern yourself with the latest exercise rage or what's in vogue. Do what you enjoy and what's right for you. That way you'll stick to it.

Setting goals

Now it's time for you to set yourself some goals in this area. I'm going to take you through your health form in more detail and show you how to incorporate the information, useful hints and little goals in this chapter.

Exercise

HEALTH

Goals

1. Improve my appearance and change my image.

2. Eat a healthy diet.

3. Exercise more.

Little goals

1. Book a hair appointment today.

2. Eat five portions of fruit and vegetables today.

3. Walk to work.

Personal strengths

1. I have worked through all the previous chapters in this book and am getting in the habit of setting little goals every day and making small changes.

2. I know how important it is to eat a healthy diet.

3. I love the difference it makes to my body and how I feel when I exercise more.

Immediate challenges/blocks/problems

1. I hate shopping for clothes.

2. I don't like cooking and always use convenience meals.

3. I get bored quickly with exercising.

Development skills

1. Decide on a style I want and plan in advance what I want to buy rather than wandering aimlessly round clothes shops.

2. Plan meals in advance and buy a recipe book with easy-cook healthy meals.

3. Change my association with exercise and see it as being fun and play time.

Achievements

I've improved my self-esteem and now have the confidence to change my image, take care of my body and get in great shape.

Filling in your form

Spend a few minutes reading through the above sample form. You will see that each section in the form is specific to the goals that have been set. For example, goal no. 2 (eat a healthy diet), is backed up by personal strength no. 2 (I know how important it is to eat a healthy diet). Then a relevant problem is identified in immediate challenges/blocks/problems no. 2 (I don't like cooking and always use convenience meals). A solution is offered in development skills no. 2 (plan meals in advance and buy a recipe book with easy-cook healthy meals). Ensure that your form follows through in the same way.

If you have been following through with your little goals, you should be seeing an improvement in your life chart (see Chapter 1). Give yourself a score that best reflects how you feel, and compare it to your original score.

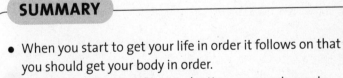

	Low								High	
Health	1	2	3	4	5	6	7	8	9	10

Keep adding those little goals to your daily diary and you'll be well on the way to achieving a high score!

SUMMARY

- When you start to get your life in order it follows on that you should get your body in order.
- Looking good doesn't have to be time consuming or to become an obsession.
- Attractiveness is a state of mind. What a person thinks of themselves, the image they have and the message they give out are often more important.

- When you warm to a personality, even their imperfections become attractive.
- We don't judge a book by its cover when we get to know someone.
- Appearance matters and by taking care of yours you'll feel better about yourself.
- You can get pampering and relaxing treatments on a shoestring from local colleges.
- Eat a healthy diet and exercise, and you'll look and feel better and years younger, and have the energy to live life to the full.
- Fill in the health section on your life chart.

10.

Organising your money

WHEN I WAS GIVING A seminar a few years ago, I asked the audience, 'What do you fear most in life?' A gentleman in the audience shouted out, 'Receiving my bank statement!' The room erupted into laughter and heads started to nod. It was obvious he'd struck a chord.

Money obviously isn't everything, but by reading this book you've signalled that you value *every* area of your life, and money is an important part of that. In this chapter, we start by discussing common attitudes towards financial problems. Then we look at how you can achieve a healthy and relaxed attitude towards money. I ask you to assess your current financial status and review your income and expenditure. Finally, we use the 10 per cent approach to help you set goals, and organise and take control of your finances.

Two attitudes: hide and speak

When clients discuss their financial problems there are two common attitudes: the first is *hide*. This is where there is a lot of shame and I'm given information on a strictly 'need to know basis'. The second is *speak*, where the client wants to put all the cards on the table and talk at length.

Case study

Rosemary wanted to 'speak'. She was a twenty-nine-year-old PR consultant with a bad spending habit. She brought me her bank statements, demand letters, credit card bills and a list of all her outgoings as proof. 'It's such a relief to be able to *tell* someone how *bad* my financial situation is,' she said with a sigh. 'I'll happily pay you to sort things out for me.'

Rosemary was maxing out on her credit cards and travelling across town every day in taxis. I was able to point out to her that travelling to business meetings by taxi in London traffic was both costly and time consuming. I said that the Tube was a quicker and cheaper option. She flicked her hand up to my face, and said, 'Stop there. I don't do Tubes.'

Rosemary defended her every financial transaction and extravagance, and it soon became apparent that while she was willing to spend the *whole day* talking, she wasn't willing to change the way she handled money.

While I *can* make practical suggestions to clients, ultimately the truth is that only you hold the power, and the best attitude is to want to learn how to use that power wisely. You have to be prepared to change the way you do things when there's a problem with your finances. There's no quick-fix solution, and you can't carry on doing what you've always done.

Another client, Ben, was the opposite of Rosemary: he was a hider.

Case study

Ben was a twenty-six-year-old freelance photographer. The very mention of finances caused him to lower his head in a posture of shame. His voice would trail off in mid-sentence and he would massage his temples as though he was soothing a pounding headache.

Finances *were* a headache for Ben, and he felt embarrassed and humiliated that his were in such a mess. Getting him to disclose the extent of his problem took very gentle coaching and constant reassurance that I wasn't going to give him a lecture or reprimand him like a naughty schoolboy. He said, 'You must think I'm such an idiot. I bet you've never had a client whose finances are so chaotic.'

I explained to Ben that money management is a much-neglected skill and few people have even the basics. Sure, they can add up and subtract, but that's not the same skill as running a household budget or managing their own finances. However bad you think your situation is, there are thousands of people in a similar position. Feeling inadequate or inept won't improve your situation, whereas taking action *will*.

Ben was willing to make the necessary changes to get his finances in order. He consolidated his debts by taking out one manageable loan. He also made a commitment *not to overspend* in the future. To help him do this he worked to a monthly budget and destroyed all his credit cards.

Why people get into debt

Attempting to realise your lifestyle goals by using credit cards is the major reason why people get into debt. I speak from experience. I've spent money I don't have and later paid the price. Soon after turning twenty I found myself wanting a nice car and a wardrobe full of designer clothes. I was seduced by easy credit and ran up outrageous bills on my credit and store cards. The result? I had to sell the car because I couldn't afford the driving lessons, and the clothes were out of fashion by the time I'd finished paying for them.

I *do* understand what it's like to want a bit of 'retail therapy'. Clothes often make us *look* better and (more importantly) *feel* better about ourselves. However, recreational shopping is all too often a quick fix to reward ourselves, or else a means to compensate ourselves for the more important things in life we are lacking.

Whether it's a high-street fashion buy, a new car, a pasta maker or a holiday – be aware that exceeding your limit is all too easy to do. With so much on offer, achieving a better lifestyle has never been so tempting.

Once debt begins to accumulate, it's an indication that you are losing control of your finances and pursuing a lifestyle you can't afford. There's nothing wrong with wanting a better lifestyle, but you won't achieve it on credit. When you have sleepless nights worrying about how you'll keep up with the payments, you won't find yourself enjoying any of the purchases you make.

Avoiding debt

If you have lifestyle goals such as making more money, having a bigger house or buying a new car, you must have your financial house in order before pursuing them. Therefore, if your finances need to be organised, a good goal to begin with is taking control of your finances and staying in credit. Once you achieve this goal, you can pursue your other goals safe in the knowledge that you'll be achieving them without jeopardising your financial position.

One of the most common forms of debt is overspending on credit cards. If you honestly believe you *can't* trust yourself with them, then avoid them. That could be your goal for today – cutting up all your credit and store cards.

If you feel you *can* manage credit cards, subscribe to one with a low interest rate. There are some good deals on the market, and although many customers are paying as much as 20 per cent interest there are much lower rates available. If you feel you are paying too much interest, phone up your credit card company and tell them you are thinking of transferring to another card with a better rate. My experience is that they will offer to match the competition rather than lose you as a customer.

There are cards available where you pay no interest on transfers for a stated period (normally six months). When that period expires you can switch to another card or ask for a better rate.

Watch out for store cards! Their rates are normally much higher than those on normal credit cards, so unless you pay off your balance within the interest-free period you could end up being stung.

Debt recovery is an enormously expensive process, and this

makes most loan companies far more sympathetic than you may realise. Debts can be frozen and manageable repayment schemes can be negotiated. However, you have to be brave enough to face the facts, pick up the phone and let the companies know what's happening. Having your mind put at rest may only be a phone call away.

A word of caution about debt consolidation: many people are tempted by the idea of one manageable monthly payment. However, this often involves switching from an unsecured loan to a secured loan. If you put up your home as security, you risk losing the roof over your head. Shop around and make sure you are not paying high interest rates or taking out payment protection insurance with unfair terms. A normal unsecured loan with competitive rates is what you should aim for.

Clients often ask me if they should start a saving plan *before* paying off debts. As a general rule it's usually best to pay off debts first. This is because the amount of interest you pay on your debts almost always exceeds any income from savings. You also have to factor in the amount of tax you will have to pay on savings. Get advice on your personal circumstances. There are registered charities that can help you cope with the stress and work out a debt-management strategy.

Taking control of your finances

Negative emotions about finance aren't governed just by how much or how little money you have, but also by the level of control you feel you have. Once you feel in control of a situation, you get the power and this allows you to see what choices you have.

While Ben (see page 140) did have a problem with his finances (more money going out than coming in), his other real and immediate concern was that he felt crippled by the lack of control of his finances and this was preventing him from addressing the issue.

Clients often tell me that they would have more choices in life if they had more money, but that's not always the case. I've coached enough high-income earners to know that if they haven't acquired good money-management skills or made a positive association with finances, they continue to experience negative emotions about their finances and feel they have limited choices.

High earners usually have high overheads, and while money can buy you a better quality of life it can also buy you a lot of stuff that needs to be maintained: the second house in the country, a boat and expensive school fees. When you look at their ratio of income and expenditure they can be right up to the line, leaving very limited disposable income.

Achieving a healthy balance

We've all met people who *never* seem satisfied with life. Whatever they get they always want more, and they're preoccupied to the point of obsession with people who have more than they do. These people are always chasing the next carrot: a new car, a computer upgrade or the latest fashion.

This state of mind comes about when you're not clear about what you want from life. If you read the above paragraph and thought, *that's me*, perhaps you should stop thinking: *What can I buy now that will make me happy?* Take a step back and ask yourself: *What are my priorities and values? What will really make me happy?*

Money has its rewards, but it is best enjoyed when you aim to have balance in your life, along with goals and aspirations for all of the seven life areas. Placing too much emphasis on money and pinning all your hopes and dreams on what it can bring will never make you happy.

Having clear ideas about where you are going in life and what you want to achieve will help you keep your finances in perspective – for example, if you value financial security but want a new kitchen, the direction you will go in is to save up for it rather than get it on credit. Having that new kitchen today would be great, but if you know that being in debt causes you problems, an upgrade won't make you happy if it means sacrificing peace of mind.

A small goal today could be to read through the list of values you identified in Chapter 3 and remind yourself what's *really* important to you.

Exercise

I would like you to answer the following list of questions in your diary. By doing so you can put some ground rules in place and establish the direction you want to go in with your finances. Your answers will help you to set appropriate goals later in the chapter.

- How much money would be enough?

- Am I happy with my current financial situation?

- What are the major financial problems I face? (List them.)

- What am I doing to change/improve the situation?

- Am I spending beyond my means?

- Do I work to a monthly budget?

- Am I planning for the future, i.e. pension schemes, life insurance and savings?

- Do I enjoy my money?

- What changes am I prepared to make to improve my financial situation?

Assessing your financial position

Now you are going to calculate your monthly income and out-goings. When I do this exercise with clients I'm constantly staggered by how inaccurate the initial figures are! To help you take *everything* into account, I have provided a list of things to help jog your memory.

The first section is items that have to be covered and are necessary expenditures. The second section includes all items that are not crucial. You should restrict yourself to two lists because there will be some items you may think you *can't* live without, like cigarettes, the latest mobile phone or membership of a gym. However, you have to achieve an *accurate* figure for *necessary* spending to calculate an accurate amount left over for choice purchases.

Exercise

Section 1

Mortgage/rent

Amenities, i.e. gas, electricity, water rates, telephone

Council tax

Service charges

Travel expenses

Food

Standing orders

Credit card/loan repayments

Car tax, petrol, insurance, parking, car loan

Household maintenance

House and contents insurance

Medical insurance

Life insurance

Pension plan

Childcare

Pet care

(If your amenity bills are quarterly work out the monthly average)

Section 2

Entertainment, i.e. cinema, eating out, socialising

Takeaways

Recreational habits, i.e. smoking, drinking

Clothes

Gym membership

Subscriptions

Magazines, newspapers

CDs, videos, DVDs

Hair care

Mobile telephone

Hobbies

You can break this exercise down into the 10 per cent approach by making a note of your expenditure every day for a month. When there are several people in the household listing all expenditures, major and minor, over a month will give you the most accurate results.

Without fail, my clients are surprised at their results and an immediate bonus is that they can always see areas to make savings on. It could be reducing your takeaway bill, cancelling a subscription to a magazine you never read or shopping in bulk so that you aren't always rushing out to the late-night (and expensive) corner shop.

Financial planning

If I asked you to fill your car with petrol and keep driving until you ran out of fuel, I'm sure you'd think that was a ludicrous request. After all, you could end up stranded in the middle of nowhere! But hang on a minute: my ludicrous request is exactly what many people do with their finances. They have little idea of their living expenses and just keep spending until they run out of money. Then they acquire credit and start spending again until they hit their limit. You've taken the time to calculate your expenditure, so that already puts you ahead of the game. Like my analogy of the car journey, you know how much money you have got coming in and how far it has to go. It therefore makes sense to have a budget.

Allocating a budget is the key to financial planning. Making 'impulse buys' results in overspending and debt. A budget will set a limit for you, and you can choose what areas and items are your priority spends. To begin with, you may find it easier to implement a budget using the 10 per cent approach and selecting one area. For example, if luxury food or drink items – like pâté or expensive wines – are costing you a lot more money every month than you realised, you may want to cut back here first.

By making one small change, you'll see that you can make a difference and follow a sensible plan. You can also set lots of little goals that will increase your money-management skills and keep your finances in order. We're about to start work on your goals, but before I move on to them I'd like you to locate your financial life chart, which has a section for goals, personal strengths, immediate challenges/blocks, development skills and achievements.

I'll take you through each section of the form and give you examples of goals for this area and how to fill in your finances form.

Exercise

FINANCES

Goals

Work to a monthly budget.

Start a pension plan.

Save 10 per cent of my salary.

Fill in my chequebook stubs.

Allocate time every week to review my spending.

Little goals

Start listing my daily expenditure.

Make enquiries about better mortgage deals.

Get information on pension plans.

Remember to keep your goals positive and relevant to what you want to achieve. The goal section isn't the place to highlight a problem, e.g. stop overspending.

Personal strengths

I have saved up for things in the past.

I'm committed to taking control of my finances.

I enjoy my money.

I keep money in perspective.

I have a pension plan.

I make it a priority to pay all the bills.

Immediate challenges/blocks/problems

I have debts.

I don't earn enough money.

My outgoings are very high.

I have a bad credit rating.

What you put in this section will determine what you have to do next to solve your problem. For example, if you are in debt then getting good advice is imperative. You can contact a Citizens Advice Bureau, which gives free advice, or alternatively find one of the many debt-counselling charities, which you can locate through your local library. If your outgoings are very high, you can decide what areas to cut back on.

Development skills

Get some financial advice.

Buy some books on the subject.

Become less concerned about keeping up with others.

Remind myself every day what my priorities are so I'm not tempted by impulse purchases.

Achievements

I've learned that money isn't everything.

I've saved for a holiday this year.

I've reduced my debts.

I switched mortgages and got a much better deal.

I prioritise my spending.

When you set goals in your financial area, make sure that the rest of your form follows on with relevant comments in each section. An example follows.

- **Goals** If your goal is to save 10 per cent of your salary every month, this would be supported by the following:

- **Personal strength** I have saved money in the past. Then you should identify a problem that is stopping you achieving your goal, like:

- **Immediate challenges/blocks/problems** I am overspending every month. Now look for a skill that would remove the problem and help you to achieve your goal, such as:

- **Development skills** Prioritise my spending and stick to a budget so I'm not tempted by impulse purchases.

Finally, you need to stay motivated, and that's why listing your achievements – however minor – is *essential*.

Make the difference today by doing something. Here is a reminder of the small goals identified in this chapter, as well as some additional ones.

- Organise a space to keep your bills and arrange them in a folder.

- Save up to go on holiday.

- Save 10 per cent of your salary.

- Switch to a better mortgage deal.

- Use Internet banking to monitor all your transactions.

- Check all your standing orders to ensure that you are not paying for something you don't need or use, like a magazine subscription or gym membership.

- Get some information on a pension scheme.

- Fill in your chequebook stubs.

- Dispense with any credit and store cards.

- Shop around for the best interest rates and loans.

- Pick up the phone and let a company know what's happening if you can't keep up with repayments.

- Start listing your daily expenditure so that you have an accurate idea of your spending.

- Read your list of values.

- If you do take out a credit card, subscribe to one with a low or no interest rate.

- Allocate one area you will budget in.

- Get some expert advice from the Citizens Advice Bureau or one of the charity debt-counselling organisations.

Do a little bit every day and in a few weeks' time you'll be benefiting from taking control of and organising your finances.

Now it's time to assess how your score is improving on your financial life chart.

	Low								High	
Finance	1	2	3	4	5	6	7	8	9	10

SUMMARY

- To keep your finances in perspective you have to take control of and manage them.
- You hold the power to manage your finances, and the best attitude to take is to learn how to use the power wisely.
- When you have a problem managing your finances, you have to be prepared to do things differently.
- You can't achieve a better lifestyle on credit.
- Accumulating debt is an indication that you are losing control and pursuing a lifestyle you can't afford.
- You have to get your financial house in order before pursuing lifestyle goals.
- Avoid credit cards if you can't trust yourself with them; avoid paying high interest rates on credit and store cards.
- When you take control of your finances, you'll find it easier to achieve a healthy and relaxed attitude towards money.
- You need to know your income and expenditure to budget wisely.
- Set goals in your financial chart and do something today.

11.

Being happy and successful at work

Y OUR WORK SHOULD GIVE you a sense of achievement and be a means to express yourself, and it can also be central to your social life. It may represent your public identity and be pivotal to your self-esteem. Getting it right is essential to your well-being.

In this chapter I focus on methods of increasing your happiness and success in the workplace. To warm up we look at preparing yourself for the workplace. Then you can roll your sleeves up and get out your diary, at which point you learn to love the job you have – this includes ideas and practical exercises to help you deal with change, and also make your professional relationships more harmonious. Finally, we look at ways in which you can identify your dream job and get it.

Three words of warning: do not skip any of the sections in this chapter. You may now be thinking: *I can skip the section on learning to love the job I have because I need to find a job I love!* However, the two are linked: work through the whole chapter and all will be revealed.

Preparing yourself for work

Our parents and teachers were the first people to shape our attitudes towards work. There is a good chance that while you were in your teens you will have been encouraged to opt for a job that provided security, status or a good salary. Perhaps you were guided (or pushed) into doing a job you were *capable* of rather than *suitable* for. However, being capable of doing a job doesn't necessarily mean that the job will suit you, allow you to express yourself or – indeed – fire your passion.

Passion is a word that you may think is more suited to films like *Last Tango in Paris* or *9½ Weeks*, rather than associated with work. I can understand this: I used to think of work as being hard graft, toil and labour – but it needn't be and shouldn't be.

There's every reason to feel optimistic about entering the workplace today, with so many opportunities available. Being employed may suit you, or alternatively you may want to spread your entrepreneurial wings in anything from party planning and IT training to pet sitting.

Case study

My friend Kelvin started his working life scanning groceries in a supermarket. He says, 'Every second robbed me of a piece of my soul.' But Kelvin lived for the buzz he got from skimming the waves on his surfboard. Like so many people, Kelvin thought of work as a necessary evil that you needed to do in order to pay the bills. Several months into a soul-destroying job, he realised that there was nothing stopping him from turning his passion into a career by training as a surf instructor.

Today, twelve years on, Kelvin spends the summers teaching surfing (at my local beach in Cornwall), and when the weather turns cold he teaches snowboarding in France. He also organises sporting adventure holidays and an event called Surfstock, which attracts people from all over Britain.

Wait a minute – what am I saying; what am I telling you? That we should all give up our jobs, buy a VW camper, wax a surfboard and move to the coast to set up a surfing school? No – at least not yet. My point is that you can achieve your goals in the workplace.

The new life/big jump approach worked for Kelvin. For other people small, purposeful steps work better. Why? The common scenario is that you plan to make a big jump one day, but the next day the distance to be crossed looks too great and you fall back on your old routines. The 10 per cent approach shows you how to bridge that gap.

Let's take a look at your work/career form. This chapter will help you to formalise your goals and set little goals. Here is an example of a completed form.

Exercise

WORK/CAREER

Goals

Get more enjoyment from my work.

Get along better with difficult work colleagues.

Switch off from work at the end of my working day.

Little goals

Select a task at work today and give it my full attention.

Make a conscious effort to be less affected by someone at work today.

Allocate a time when I will switch off from work today and find something relaxing to do.

Personal strengths

I enjoy many aspects of my job.

I am hard-working and reliable.

I am willing to try a new approach.

Immediate challenges/blocks/problems

I take on too much work and then get stressed and irritable.

I have alienated some of my work colleagues by letting lots of minor things build up – then I blow my fuse.

I spend way too much time thinking about work in the evenings and churning myself up over misunderstandings.

Development skills

I need to learn to organise my work better and not over-commit myself.

I need to learn how to express myself better and deal with things as they come up rather than let them build up.

I need to learn how to relax more after work and find interesting hobbies and activities.

Achievements

I have mastered all the new technology that has been introduced at work and kept up with all the training courses.

I have secured several large orders for the company.

I successfully negotiated a pay rise.

Now I'll show you how to achieve the goals set out in the sample form.

Get ready to enjoy work

Learning to get the most from a job – even one you don't like – eliminates the risk of forming a negative association about the very nature of work. Deep down, some individuals harbour the belief that work isn't something they're *meant* to enjoy. So even if their job is good 90 per cent of the time, they'll leave work every day demoralised by the 10 per cent they don't like.

Life always conspires to support our beliefs. So if you consider work to be dull, boring and stressful, you will start to lack the motivation to improve your lot. Your working day will constantly confirm the negative views you hold and will drag out for an eternity. You will start to become locked into a five-day downward spiral that starts with *I don't like Mondays* and ends with *Thank God it's Friday!*

However, someone who sees work as a form of self-expression and is committed to a positive vision of their working life can find fulfilment and happiness in the workplace.

Learning to love the job you do

Relationships with friends, partners and family often need a lot of time, work and effort. Your relationship with your job is exactly the same. There is so much change in the workplace now that we can confuse disliking our job with disliking the changes within our job – there's a big difference. One of my clients, David, came to see me asking for career tips.

Case study

David had just turned forty-one and was working as a senior hospital doctor. Like most senior doctors, he had struggled through years of training and a lot of very long hours to get to the position he was now in. But David was having doubts about his job. 'It's just not exciting me in the way it used to,' he said.

After talking to David for half an hour, I found that he was actually happy with and indeed passionate about his job. However, he was *unhappy* with the paperwork that recent changes had created. 'And also,' he said, 'I'm struggling to get along with a couple of people I work with.'

Here was the nub of the matter: for David the problem was *not* the job itself, but changes and people within the job that were starting to make his day unpleasant. The answer was *not* to get a new career, *or* to go and work in a new department. David had to work on his people skills, develop his ability to handle office politics and learn how to delegate his paperwork.

David is typical of the numerous people who come to me saying that they are unhappy with their jobs. Many have spent years hopping from career to career and job to job without finding happiness, not because it has been the *job itself* that has been wrong, but the *elements within it*.

The most common complaints I hear from clients include: personality clashes, doing endless menial tasks, an inability to switch off after work, office politics, favouritism, a lack of respect and/or appreciation. Do any of these ring bells for you? If they do, before you consider looking for a new job let's first see if we can get your old job to work better for you.

Developing the right attitude

Even when you accept that a change of attitude is needed, adjusting can still be difficult. Having goals provides an excellent way of developing your attitude because they require you to focus on what you want and take action. It's only through *positive actions* that you can form *positive beliefs*.

I'm going to help you to form positive beliefs by suggesting little goals that immediately improve the quality of your working day. You can select the goals in any order, but do try all of them. By achieving these daily goals you will develop key skills that allow you to get more enjoyment from your existing job, pursue a promotion or move into a career that you feel more suited to.

Goal: select one of your work tasks and give it your undivided attention as you perform it For example, if there's some tedious filing or a lengthy report to be written, concentrate all your efforts into doing that job to the *best* of your ability. Monitor how you feel and how time flies when you put 100 per cent effort into a job. You'll feel more relaxed because dividing your attention causes tension, whereas directing it in one area allows you to relax. Absorbing yourself in the moment makes a job satisfying.

Goal: allocate a time to cut yourself off from work Work often encroaches on your time and mind a lot more than you realise. Learning to switch off allows you to relax and recharge. After work finishes, you must have no work-related conversations and deflect any work-related thoughts from your mind. It's not as easy as it sounds, but it's well worth achieving, so stick with it. Try turning off a work mobile phone or changing your clothes at the end of your working day (especially if you wear a uniform or have to dress formally).

Goal: only say positive things and have positive thoughts You'll have to constantly monitor your thoughts to keep them positive. Don't join in any negative conversations with work colleagues or acknowledge negative remarks about others.

Goal: make a note in your diary of all the compliments, thank yous and praise you receive You'll need to be vigilant because you probably miss or quickly dismiss words of praise or a simple thank you. So whether it's a thank you for holding the lift, a compliment about what you're wearing, or an acknowledgement of a job well done – make a note. You'll be pleasantly surprised at how many compliments you've stacked up at the end of the day. Moreover, if you make it a game to try and get as many compliments as possible, you'll have a great working day.

Goal: speak your mind about something you've been holding back on There is always some aspect of the workplace that causes you an ongoing niggling problem. Follow these guidelines on being assertive, but avoid unpleasant confrontation.

1. Be clear about what you want to achieve. That way you won't simply tell someone what the problem is. You'll also be able to offer a solution that would work for you. For example, if a work colleague constantly takes their lunch break at the busiest time of the day and you're left to man the phones and deal with all the work, suggest times that would be more acceptable for their

lunch break and then explain the problem with the existing arrangement.

2. Always express yourself in a positive way. Don't raise your voice, and highlight why a situation causes you a problem – for example, explain that a deadline is too short to produce the high standard of work you want to deliver. Refrain from ever being personal or sounding critical – for example, telling someone that they are disorganised or never listen to anyone, or that you can never get a decision out of them.

3. Set yourself a time limit for a conversation and stick to it. The golden rule to being assertive is knowing when to stop.

Practising positive assertiveness is an imperative skill in the workplace, and however challenging you find it you'll feel a lot better saying what you want to say than suffering in silence.

Goal: remind yourself of the purpose of your work Whether you work in the public or private sector, for a business that produces goods or services, or are self-employed – identify the purpose of what you do. My client Lee worked as a waiter in a restaurant. He had identified his purpose when he said, 'I work in the service sector providing food and beverages. My customers are mainly holidaymakers, and my purpose is to make them feel welcome, provide a fast and efficient service, be on hand to cater to all their needs and be a memorable part of their holiday experience.' With that sense of purpose, Lee really enjoys his job.

Goal: write a positive affirmation about your work today and use it throughout the day The power of an affirmation is generated by constant repetition, which establishes the message in the subconscious mind. Let's say that you write the affirmation: 'I am enjoying my work more and more and am finding it more and more rewarding.' This is a good affirmation because you are working to a state of more enjoyment. Even if you are experiencing discontent, your focus is on improving and upgrading how you feel.

Once you familiarise yourself with these seven goals, you can build up to a point where you are using all of them every day. Over time they will become second nature, and you'll find they have a major impact on the quality of your working day.

Master class in managing people

I hope you've begun to realise that the one person who controls the way you feel is you. Yes, there might be bullying bosses, surly subordinates and uncooperative colleagues, but ultimately you control your own feelings.

To survive the hotbed of difficult personalities that can be found in every workplace – yes, every workplace – you need the right skills. These skills won't make a difficult person reasonable, a dishonest person honest or a mean boss generous. What they will do is make your working life easier. The following little goals can help you achieve a very common big goal, which is to have happy and successful relationships with work colleagues.

Goal: I'm going to identify a difficult work colleague who has helped me to achieve something I wanted Let's say your boss is an overbearing oaf – but has his manner pushed you to improve in an area, develop new skills or improve your own ability to manage people? Difficult personalities don't necessarily get in the way of you achieving something.

I want you to spend a few minutes thinking about this, because when you start to find positives in difficult personalities your ability to manage and deal with them is immediately increased. When you can see a gain, focus on this, rather than feeling stressed or drained by their behaviour.

Goal: I'm going to make a conscious effort today to be less affected by someone It's easy to say, 'Don't let them get to you' or 'Just ignore them.' But when you've got them breathing down your neck all day or always finding fault, the bottom line is that they *do* get to you. The first action to take is to recognise what is happening and how it affects you. This will indicate how best to deal with it and what small steps you can start to take. So if they make your blood boil, use anger-management techniques like taking a brisk walk or breathing deeply. Remind yourself what it is you're trying to achieve and you could find that they're not getting in your way as much as you first thought.

Goal If you ever feel inadequate and doubt your ability at work, use your diary to weigh up the pros and cons of a situation and see if your feelings are rational and justified. In short, identify the *real problem* instead of taking it personally.

Goal: I'm going establish a boundary at work today You know when someone has crossed the line, but they may not. If you smile sweetly when someone makes an inappropriate comment or immediately agree to work through a lunch hour, but are quietly seething, then it's an indication that you find it hard to communicate your boundaries. A lot of people struggle in this area mainly because they want to avoid confrontation, causing upset or being badly thought of. However, here's something to remember: confrontation is unavoidable, and handled correctly can be a good thing.

Establishing boundaries is one of the tools of assertiveness, and it's ultimately *your* responsibility to communicate what is and what isn't acceptable. However much you dislike doing it, I can guarantee you'll dislike the feeling of not doing it a lot more. You'll avoid those repetitive conversations in your head about what you should have said and wanted to say, those feelings of frustration and being undermined, the overwhelming sense of unfairness.

Start with the small stuff and I promise you that the more you practise the easier it gets. It could be as simple as asking someone not to use your mug, or to return items they are always borrowing from your desk.

I would like you to pause now for a few minutes. I've given you a lot of information and little goals. However, this is a big topic and I want you to appreciate just how many things you can do to change your working day. If you have completed your work/career form there will be several little goals that are relevant to you in the section we have just covered, so take out your diary and select five little goals that you are willing to commit to. Now work those little goals into your weekly schedule.

Getting the job you love

If you've applied the previous goals and techniques, your working day will definitely improve. However, if you've analysed, persevered and honed your people skills and things are still not working for you, the time has come to find a job you love.

I know the feeling of being a square peg in a round hole. I was just eighteen when I started my first 'real' job as a nursing assistant in a geriatric hospital. On the day I started I had to dress and feed several immobile and incontinent male patients. A few days later I had to assist in laying out a dead body. The world of work felt brutal and I wanted to escape to a career that was glamorous and fun.

I had made the mistake of thinking that a vocational job like nursing would give me a personal sense of purpose. After all, it was a *good* job and by doing it I'd be a *good* person. So I knuckled down, overcame my fears and tried very hard. I didn't want to let my family down or feel like a failure by walking away from something because I found it hard. However, the bottom line was that it always felt like hard work because I was doing a job that I wasn't suited to. I left after two years feeling relieved, but having no idea what I wanted to do.

After several years of job-hopping I asked myself the vital questions: *What is the purpose of my working life and what do I want to achieve?* After asking myself those two questions, my whole attitude towards work changed. Rather than be a passive employee waiting for the job to deliver what I needed, I had to identify what it was I was looking for and actively seek it.

Once you uncover your purpose and know what you're looking for, your dream job is a lot easier to find. You no longer rely on luck and start to act on judgement. So instead of waiting for things to fall into place or the right job to materialise, you think: *What is it I want to do? What type of work would allow me to express myself and give me a sense of achievement?*

There are challenges in every type of job. Some involve life-and-death decisions, others test you academically or stretch your self-esteem. A physically demanding job can make you question your fitness or age. Job satisfaction comes from overcoming a challenge that is worthwhile to you on a personal level.

Good job, bad job

Clients often ask me what I consider to be a good job. My answer is always, 'A good job is one that suits you and makes you happy.' I don't reel off a list of good jobs, because I don't believe there is a category of what constitutes a good job or a bad job. My dad spent most of his working life in a dark, damp coalmine with a shovel in his hand. I never once heard him complain. For him, hard graft satisfied his work ethic.

I've heard plenty of people complain about jobs that most of us would think are cushy numbers, and have also heard plenty of people motivated and enthusiastic about a job that would be challenging to the average person.

As I mentioned earlier, the secret of the right job *isn't* the job itself. Every job has its challenges, but they have to be significant to you and satisfy your personal sense of purpose.

Finding the right job

Successful career changes don't occur overnight. It can take six months to a year and it *should* because getting it right – finding a job you are suited to – is a major life decision. I want you to take the pressure off yourself to come up with the perfect job overnight. A much better approach is to build up a career portfolio, and to gather information about different jobs and the world of work. This approach worked for one of my clients.

Case study

Twenty-five-year-old Adam had a degree in English and came to me wondering what to do next. He'd mulled over the idea of becoming a teacher, but it wasn't something that really excited him. So he'd ended up working for a market research company to earn some money. 'It's just a stop-gap,' he said. 'I don't want to end up doing this for the rest of my life.'

For the first ten minutes of our session, every time I asked him what he wanted to do, he'd say, 'Dunno.' Then I said to him, 'Well if you *did know* – what would it be?' Adam replied, 'A television producer – maybe.' Then he glanced around the room as if surprised by where his answer came from.

The question I asked Adam sounds like a very odd one, but it often does the trick. My theory is that people feel under such pressure or are so embarrassed about admitting their real interest that mentally they freeze. By asking an unexpected question, the brain unlocks and out pops an answer.

Adam went on to gather information about being a television producer. He put together a file on different jobs in the industry, and gathered information on the background and merits of different companies and organisations. He used his two-week summer holiday to get some work experience as a runner (general gofer) on a home-shopping channel. From there, he was able to see what areas he liked about the working environment and the different types of job that exist, and what skills are needed. Adam got the chance to try his hand at everything from set design to camera and sound work when they pre-recorded footage.

To increase his skills, Adam saved up and enrolled in several BBC training courses in production, and then secured a job with an independent production company that specialises in documentaries. The whole process took six months. Adam is now an assistant producer and he loves the job.

What I want to do now is use the 10 per cent approach and give you small, manageable goals to help you find your dream job. Remember that this can be a six-month to a year-long project, so you have plenty of time to gather your resources and implement these small goals.

Big goal: find a job I love

This big goal can be achieved by breaking it down into little goals as follows.

Read your list of values that you identified in Chapter 3 and highlight the values you want to satisfy in your working life It could be some or all of them. You might have family life as a major value and wish to work for a company that offers flexible working hours or contracts that run during school terms. If travel is something you value, you may want a job that involves travel or allows you to take your four- or six-week annual holiday in one go so that you can go backpacking for a month.

Spend five minutes every day looking at recruitment adverts in newspapers or on the Internet Browse through all the sections, reading the adverts and job descriptions, and allow your instincts to tell you what areas you feel yourself drawn to or interested in.

Start a work/career file using an A4 folder and add information to it every day You only have to add a small bit of information and spend five minutes adding to your file every day. I'll give you a list of headings to steer you in the right direction and help you compile the sort of information you'll need. Begin with the heading: 'Reasons why I work', and every time you think of a reason add it to your list. It might start with something like: 'I need to earn money', 'I need to gain recognition and be good at what I do', or 'It gives me self-respect'. Include the following headings on separate pieces of paper: 'Jobs I like the sound of',

'My strengthens and weaknesses' (include your skills and identify any areas in which you think you need new skills or additional training). Add: 'What I want from a company'. This will help you to recognise a company's culture – how things are done there, and if they offer a pension plan, good training, staff perks or a team spirit.

Gather information on a different career every week Don't just focus on jobs you like the sound of. Jobs you may have dismissed can be appealing when you know more about them. You can get information by talking to friends in different careers, using the Internet, requesting brochures from companies and visiting your local library.

Take note of what makes you happy During the course of your day, identify what activities you enjoy. Do you feel happiest being on the go, moving around and meeting lots of people? Perhaps you prefer quiet activities or academic challenges? Does loud music and a noisy atmosphere make you feel upbeat or edgy and distracted? Are your happiest moments spent with the same people? Do you like to mix with a variety of age groups? Is your preference for male or female company, or a mixture of both? What are your happiest achievements? Some individuals are happiest creating something from start to finish and have total control over the end project. Sharing in a joint venture and working as part of a team may be your preference.

The things that make you happy during your day are all essential clues to what sort of job and working environment would suit you. I love working alone, with no background noise or interruptions. My happiest moments during the day are predominantly quiet ones and ones shared with people I love. For my friend Kelvin – the surfing teacher – sitting in front of a computer all day long and working in solitude would be his idea of hell! He can't sit still, is a real adrenalin junkie and is at his happiest when his day is action-packed and people-filled.

Now I want you to refer again to your work/career form. There may be goals on it you feel ready to take action on, or you may prefer to try my suggested little goals to build up your confidence and show you just how much you can achieve by taking small steps.

To be in a job you love and feel passionate about is a wonderful feeling. You have the power to transform your working life and you owe it to yourself to make it the best it can be.

Make sure you are implementing your little goals. When you are, your score for this section will increase.

Now it's time to fill in your life chart for work/career and see how your score has improved.

	Low								*High*	
Work/career	1	2	3	4	5	6	7	8	9	10

SUMMARY

- What you do for a living matters on many levels – it's a means of expressing yourself and a part of your public identity, and it can be pivotal to your self-esteem and central to your social life.
- The new world of work offers more flexibility and opportunities than ever before.
- Life always conspires to support your beliefs. To have a happy and successful working life you need a positive attitude and positive beliefs.
- Having goals is an excellent way to develop the right attitude because you are directing both your thoughts and actions on the positive outcome you want to achieve.

- Try some of the suggested little goals to help you develop the right working attitude, deal with stress, feel empowered and find purpose in the work you do.
- You can't change difficult people, but you can manage them.
- Ask yourself: what is the purpose of my working life and what do I want to achieve?
- Start a career portfolio.
- Successful career changes don't happen overnight and can take six months to a year.
- If you are implementing your little goals, your score for work/career will go up.

12.

Making the most of family relationships

WHEN FAMILY RELATIONSHIPS work they're well worth making the effort for. The rewards like love, support and a sense of belonging are things we all *need* and want in our lives.

By contrast, when family relationships turn sour, emotions run extremely high. I'm sure you've had your own experience of family members pushing you to the limit. However close your family is, there will be at least one immediate or extended family member you find difficult to get along with. It would be easy to walk away and think 'Why bother?' However, there's a very good reason to bother, and I explain why in this chapter. I also show you seven life-changing relationship skills that will benefit *every* type of relationship you have. Once you're familiar with the seven relationship skills, we turn our attention to your family/extended family form. You'll be formalising your big goals in this area and also breaking them down into little goals. Then you can select one or more of the seven relationship skills to add to your list of development skills on your form. Finally, we look at problems specific to family relationships and how you can deal with them, using little goals to improve them.

Before we get to work I want to relay a story to you: I was on a train to London recently – trying to enjoy my chick lit book – but I couldn't block out the conversation that was going on next to me. Two women who had only just met spent *the entire five-hour journey* criticising their families. 'My mother's always interfering; she always thinks she knows best.' 'Mine is just the same,' replied the other woman. They continued to match each other story for story to the point of sounding competitive about who had the worst family life!

These two women were united in their misery. They saw family relationships as something negative which they had no control over, because fate was responsible for those relationships. They aren't alone in their attitude – but it's not an attitude I have, and as I said earlier, I'm going to explain why you should make the effort to have good family relationships.

The fact that your family is able to provoke such strong reactions emphasises how much you *do care* about these relationships. While I have no magic wand and can't change your family, I can provide you with seven essential skills to make your family relationships the best they can be. You can be on the receiving end of bad behaviour, or through no fault of your own be treated unfairly and unjustly criticised. However, when you apply the seven skills, bad relationships become the exception, and as a rule your relationships will reflect how you behave.

The seven relationship skills are:

1. The ability to listen.

2. The ability to express yourself.

3. The ability to be appropriate in a conversation or situation.

4. Having both self-awareness and an awareness of others.

5. Respecting other people's feelings and opinions.

6. The ability to recognise the basis of a relationship.

7. Having a healthy level of self-esteem and confidence.

I use the seven relationship skills for all three of the relationship forms in your life chart, that is family/extended family, friends/

social life and personal relationships. However, in this chapter we concentrate on how the seven relationship skills specifically relate to family relationships.

Applying the seven skills

Skill 1: the ability to listen

This is a crucial skill, and one I've mentioned in other chapters. Here are some goals that will improve your ability to listen.

Little goal: concentrate on what the *other* person is saying, rather than thinking about what *you* want to say

Little goal: ask questions so you are clear about what some- one is actually saying Questions not only demonstrate that you are listening, but also provide a platform for clearing up unnecessary misunderstandings. When talking to family we all too often run with half the information, assuming we know what is being said.

Skill 2: the ability to express yourself

You may find it easy to express yourself with some family mem- bers and not with others. However, the ideal is being able to express yourself in *any situation* and with *any family member*.

Little goal: write down what you want to say and achieve in advance As you know, I'm a firm believer in writing things down, especially when you're dealing with emotive subject mat- ter. It's very easy to say all the wrong things and way more than you wanted to say. Writing stuff down reminds you of your objective, and you will quickly see if you're being too emotional or critical.

Little goal: check your body language so that you're not giving out mixed signals If you want to have an honest conversation, you need to make eye contact to convey your sincerity. Folding your arms in a defensive position gives the impression of holding back and being guarded.

Skill 3: the ability to be appropriate in a conversation or situation

When you have an easy relationship with a family member conversations flow. You can dip in and out of different subjects, and you can turn the tables on someone without causing offence. For example, I was having a conversation with my sister Teresa (who is a teacher), and she was saying how children need to be more organised and should not turn up at school without the right books or PE kit. I reminded her of the time *she* turned up at school (she was only five, by the way) without the right costume for the school nativity play. The teacher announced 'Hark the Archangel Gabriel appeared' and Teresa glided out from the wings with arms outstretched in a saintly gesture, a halo above her angelic face, silky white dress and bottle-green woolly tights! We both had a good laugh at our childhood memory.

Little goal: leave the past behind If relationships are not harmonious, don't attempt to make a point by referring to a previous situation – stick to the subject matter. You'll know if you are *not* being appropriate when you hear a comment like, 'Trust you to drag that up again.' It's the conversation equivalent of all roads lead to Rome, but in this case all conversations lead to an argument!

Little goal: be clear about your objective If there is a sensitive issue you need to raise, do it at an appropriate time. Don't spoil a perfectly good conversation by suddenly changing the subject and putting someone on the spot. You could have the objective to begin with some light conversations. Then, when the lines of communication are flowing more easily, suggest a time to talk and tackle more serious issues.

Skill 4: having both self-awareness and an awareness of others

Are you self-aware? Do you have a fairly accurate idea of how you come across to others? If you frequently feel misunderstood, snubbed or surprised by how people react, there is a good chance that you're *not* self-aware. Try asking family members, close friends or work colleagues how you come across. What *you* see as a professional manner might be perceived by others as a cold, distant manner. What you think of as your quiet, reflective moods might be interpreted as being moody and sulky.

My client Lawrence had to address how he came across after his wife chastised him for his boardroom-speak at the dinner table. He actually asked his children for a progress report and if there were any new items on the agenda! Not surprisingly, his ten- and twelve-year-old sons were unresponsive.

Little goal: ask at least two people today how you come across in a conversation or situation Resist the temptation to argue the odds with them. For example, it can be hard to hear you come across as aggressive or overly critical when you thought you were giving constructive advice. Good intentions are not enough: they need to be matched with the correct verbal communication, tone of voice and choice of phrase.

You may recall Vicky, the radio producer, who I told you about in Chapter 2. Vicky had been bullied as a child and made the decision as an adult to be assertive, have an opinion and stand her ground. She was shocked to discover that she actually behaved like a bully.

Little goal: make a list of what you consider your most obvious qualities and ask someone who knows you well if they'll also make a list It will be a pleasant surprise if they identify extra qualities, but if they're missing the ones you think you have you'll have to work harder to demonstrate them. For example, if you think you have a sense of humour, perhaps you need to laugh more or let people know you find something funny. If you think you are very patient, but it's not obvious to others, you may need to monitor how often you lose your temper or cut people off when they're talking.

Skill 5: respecting other people's feelings and opinions

Solid relationships are built when you take a *genuine interest* in other people and care enough to demonstrate a respect for their feelings and opinions.

Little goal: express your opinion without sounding judgemental or disrespectful to other people It's better to say, 'I'd love us to spend some quiet time together and have dinner on Saturday,' rather than, 'You're such a control freak. You always make plans without consulting with me first!'

Little goal: ensure that your behaviour and actions demonstrate respect for other people's feelings We're all guilty of being insensitive at times, so making a conscious effort not to be is an essential life skill. Individuals who secure good family relationships think before they act rather than have to deal with the consequences of thoughtless behaviour.

Skill 6: the ability to recognise the basis of a relationship

This sounds like an easy one, but in reality this skill is the one most commonly ignored in family relationships. While your position in a family may stay the same – for instance you remain a son or daughter – how you behave and how your parents behave towards you changes as you get older.

For family relationships to be healthy they *do* have to change over time. As an adult, you would not expect your parents to treat you like a child, and equally problems will arise if you continue behaving like a child and expecting your parents to take responsibility for your life. This was certainly the case for my client Jack.

Case study

When Jack came to see me, he said, 'I'm fed up with my mother treating me like a child. I'm a forty-six-year-old man, but she's always expressing her opinion on everything from my latest girlfriend to the clothes I wear to what I do in my social life.' If I were to tell you that Jack was constantly getting into debt and relying on his mother to bail him out – the situation suddenly looks very different. As I said to Jack, 'If you expect your mother to pick up the tab for your lifestyle, it's hardly surprising that she feels entitled to comment on what you're spending *her money* on.'

As you can see from Jack's situation, it's important to be honest with yourself about the basis of a relationship. You can't have it both ways. If you want to be treated like an adult, that means behaving like one.

Little goal: make a conscious effort to remind yourself of the basis of a relationship If you are expecting a family member to fulfil a certain role – are you fulfilling your role?

Little goal: assess relationships on evidence and experience We often assume certain individuals will give us support with no previous evidence that they have. Look for evidence to support your beliefs and expectations.

Little goal: write down what you want and can realistically expect from a relationship You may want a relationship to be more than it is. However, when you put pen to paper it's easier to detach yourself from the emotional stew and aim for achievable little goals, rather than expect a dramatic turnaround overnight.

Skill 7: having a healthy level of self-esteem and confidence

We've worked on building your self-esteem and confidence in Chapter 5. As I said there, it's an ongoing process: something you need to keep working on and monitoring. Low self-esteem and low confidence can make you needy and too demanding in a relationship. Family members can become drained by continually having to deal with insecurities and constant requests for reassurance.

Little goal: work towards keeping a healthy balance in relationships While family can be called on for support, it's important to ensure that you don't monopolise conversations with your problems.

Little goal: take responsibility for improving your self-esteem and confidence By doing this you'll avoid seeking constant approval from your family.

By applying the goals and techniques from *one* of the seven skills *each day* for the next seven days, you'll greatly improve your skills and your ability to achieve happy and successful relationships.

Now it's time to turn our attention to your family/extended family form. I have completed a sample form, and in the development skills section I have selected some of the seven skills that would help to achieve the big and little goals set.

Exercise

FAMILY/EXTENDED FAMILY

Goals

1. Have the confidence to make my own choices.

2. Give positive feedback.

3. Be honest about my feelings.

Little goals

1. Make some decisions today without running them past my family first.

2. Focus on giving more compliments today.

3. Ask for help in cooking the evening meal and clearing up so that I don't feel exhausted and put upon.

Personal strengths

1. I trust my judgement.

2. I love my family and always put their welfare first.

3. I know the importance of setting a good example.

Immediate challenges/blocks/problems

1. I'm constantly juggling to keep everybody happy and take too much responsibility for everyone's feelings.

2. I feel like a real nag and as if I'm always on everyone's case.

3. When my family leave me to do everything I feel as though they don't care about me.

Development skills

1. Be more self-sufficient (skill 7).

2. Learn to respect other people's feelings and not come over as critical (skill 5).

3. Learn to express myself better (skill 2).

Achievements

1. I've mended a long-standing rift with my mother.

2. We do lots of things together as a family.

3. I have lots of happy memories of family time.

When you set big goals for yourself in this section, read through the seven relationship skills to identify what skills could help you achieve your goals. You may find there is more than one skill required. For example, if you have a big goal to communicate better with family, all of the seven skills may have to be used.

As I mentioned at the beginning of this chapter, these seven skills are essential to *all* relationships. Take just a few minutes out of your day to think about how you can use a skill and in a few weeks' time they'll start to become automatic skills.

Don't let problems spoil family relationships

Problems have an uncanny knack of making us incompetent. Let me explain: you might jump into your car every day and successfully manoeuvre it out of the garage without a second thought. But on the day you're feeling weighed down by problems – that's the day you'll hear the grinding of metal as you scrape against the garage wall. Just as problems can have an impact on your practical skills, they can also have an impact on your relationship skills.

When I have a problem I expect my family and friends to rally round (with a bottle of Chardonnay) and listen to me moaning about what a hard day I've had, and there is nothing wrong with that. It's acceptable in relationships for your problems to take priority at certain times. However, when problems become *the main focus* of your relationships *at all times*, that vital connection you get from others can be lost. I'll explain why.

Problems can and *do* change our behaviour: we've all snapped at the wrong person because someone has upset us. For the most part, those reactions are short-lived and don't cause a problem in our relationships. However, going through life feeling constantly wounded by your problems can have a very negative impact on relationships, especially if you start to identify yourself with your problems and believe others should make an exception for you.

Taking your problems out on other people is not only destructive to relationships, but also blocks you from using and developing essential relationship skills. My client Lisa was an example of someone who was going through life wounded by her problems.

Case study

Lisa had mapped out her life with Greg, her fiancé: house in the country, two children and (as Greg was very wealthy) she'd be a stay-at-home mum.

Just two months before their wedding, Greg delivered the shattering news that he wanted to end their relationship. Fast-forward three years and Lisa was *still* saying that Greg had ruined her life, and how unfair it was that she had to work and no longer enjoyed luxury holidays or the expensive gifts Greg used to buy her.

Just as vets know to approach wounded animals with caution, Lisa's family took a similar approach. They were always walking on eggshells around her, fearing a verbal attack if they said the wrong thing. Occasionally, when they did chastise Lisa for her behaviour she would succumb to self-pity and sob like a child about the lack of sympathy and support she got.

By the time Lisa came to see me she was distraught about the fact that family and friends were avoiding her. I asked if they were *really* unsympathetic and unwilling to offer support, or was it possible that they were unwilling to tolerate unreasonable behaviour? Initially her eyes flashed with anger, but as my question sunk in she confessed, 'I have behaved badly.'

By acknowledging this, Lisa was able to see that taking her problems out on other people was sabotaging relationships with the very people that meant the most to her. The solution was to change her behaviour. I'm happy to say that she did, by working on the seven relationship skills, in particular self-awareness and awareness for others and respecting people's opinions and feelings.

Most people *will* be sympathetic when you suffer a painful experience. Those close to you will initially both understand and tolerate any negative changes in your behaviour. However, at some point they expect normal service to resume. Being in the company of someone who expects the world to revolve around them and their problems is immensely draining. You limit the number of people you can have good relationships with, and feel dissatisfied with the level of support you get.

Here are some warning signs that may reveal if you are locked into a painful experience and, as a result, are compromising your relationships.

- You find family tactless and inconsiderate towards *your* feelings.

- You feel critical towards your family because of the lack of support.

- You feel as though your family don't understand *you* and there seems to be a shortage of like-minded people around.

- In the past you were able to form strong connections with your family, but now you feel detached and distant, even from people you used to be close to.

If you can relate to these feelings, you will find the seven relationships skills invaluable for getting your relationships back on track. Here are some little goals that are also helpful.

- Remind yourself who or what made you feel bad today. This helps to avoid taking out problems on the wrong people and family are often first in the firing line.

- Allocate quality family time and do something you don't normally do. Simply spending time with family doesn't guarantee quality time. It can be good for all of you to get out of the house and your usual surroundings and do an activity like ten-pin bowling together.

- If you need support and comfort, ask for it. Even close family members won't always pick up when you feel low. It's better to let them know how you feel than to sulk or feel resentful.

- Make a list of all the positive qualities your family have. Problems can make you feel negative, and it's very easy to start projecting those negative feelings on to family and overlook all their good qualities.

When you need to talk

Some people can't stop talking about their problems and unload them on everyone they meet. There are those who do the complete opposite and *never* discuss their problems with anyone. Both extremes can cause problems in family relationships.

Case study

Joe, aged fifty-two, was a successful businessman with a chain of bars, restaurants and commercial properties. Professionally he made sound judgements. As a professional rule, he *never* discussed his personal problems with staff or customers, and after a while that rule spilt over into his private life.

When Joe came to see me, he said, 'I'm here because I'm concerned I'm losing my focus at work.' After talking for a few minutes it became clear to me that his real concern was his relationship with his wife, which he described as 'strained'. Their son had died two years ago in a car crash, and his wife was having regular counselling to deal with her grief. 'I can't see the point in talking about it,' he told me. 'After all, it won't bring him back.'

I could have encouraged Joe to talk to me about his son and that may have helped. However, this was a situation that was, in my opinion, outside the remit of coaching. My gut feeling was that Joe needed to deal with his grief and talk to his wife about it. This would best be done through a counsellor.

Joe pursued my suggestion. He called me two months later, and said, 'Thank you for pointing me in the right direction. I realise now that talking may not bring my son back, but it certainly brought my wife back to me.'

Some problems require professional help. Joe needed a counsellor to help him express himself (skill 2), and talking about his grief helped him to deal with it and make the vital connection with his wife again.

Painful emotions have a deep impact on relationships. If you want to prevent such problems from destroying existing family relationships, keep referring to the seven relationship skills.

You may already be putting 100 per cent effort into your family relationships, but the techniques I've given you in this chapter ensure that you are combining effort with skills, which ultimately produce the best results.

Let's see how your family relationships are improving.

	Low								High	
Family	1	2	3	4	5	6	7	8	9	10

SUMMARY

- Relationships are challenging, but they're well worth the effort, with rewards such as love, support and a sense of belonging.
- All happy and successful relationships require the same skills.
- Use the suggested little goals to develop the seven relationship skills.
- When you fill in your family/extended family form, look at the seven skills and see which ones would be most useful in your development skills section.
- Avoid taking out your problems on your family.
- It's acceptable in relationships for your problems to take priority at certain times.
- Unloading your problems on everyone or never discussing them with anyone are two extremes that are both counterproductive to family relationships.
- Use little goals to prevent problems from getting in the way of family relationships.
- Combine effort with the right skills and you'll achieve big results.

13.

Building solid friendships

I'M SURE THAT, LIKE ME, you vividly recall your first real friend. I met mine on my first day at school standing in the classroom looking at a sea of unfamiliar faces. Just as I was about to succumb to a moment of terror and let out a large wail – it happened. 'Do you want to be my friend? My name is Tina.' There she was, face covered in freckles and a smile from ear to ear – my new best buddy. When my mum came to pick me up at home time, Tina MaCullock and I were practically inseparable.

Having a good friend gives you a wonderful feeling. Unlike family, you get to choose your friends and you can also determine your position or role within those relationships.

In the case of family relationships, roles are defined in the sense of you being a son or daughter, a brother or sister, a mother or father. Friendships allow versatility and you can have lots of different types of friendship. For example, your friendships in the workplace may be more formal, whereas outside work you can let your hair down with friends and may also have a different group of friends through a common interest like a sport or hobby.

While friendships can run adrift, they are unlikely to sink under the same pressures, commitments and responsibilities as those you encounter in family relationships.

There is every reason to have great friendships along with a fantastic social life, and that's what this chapter is all about. You'll be using the seven relationship skills and little goals to improve friendships and your social life. We will move on to your friends/social life form, and then I'll do a bit of trouble-shooting and look at the sorts of problems that can arise in friendships. Finally, I'll show you how to set little goals that both avoid and overcome problems.

Applying the seven skills

Skill 1: the ability to listen

Our friends can be great sounding boards and we expect them to listen to us. It's often easier to tell a friend something because they aren't immediately affected by it and that makes it a lot easier for them to take our side or offer support.

It's important to listen to what a friend is really asking you for. Let me give you an example: if a friend wants to have a good moan about their partner's behaviour, you have to determine if they want an objective overview from you or if they want you to be supportive. The issue isn't whether or not their moan is justified and they're in the right. The *real* issue is what they want you, as their friend, to provide. Here are some little goals that will help you to listen to a friend.

Little goal: determine what it is a friend is asking you for If a friend just needs to talk, you'll pick up on that up very quickly. They'll often talk without pausing and their conversation may sound like a runaway train. At times like this, let them talk; all they need you to do is *listen*. If they want feedback they'll ask for it.

Little goal: distinguish between giving advice and offering support For the most part, friends are not asking you to solve their problems or even to come up with a piece of incredibly wise council. This was demonstrated to me recently in a conversation I overheard in my kitchen between two of my male friends.

Case study

Jim and Pete (not their real names) had taken charge of preparing dinner for our group of friends. Jim said, 'My little brother is a real mess at the moment. I think he's back on the gear' (drugs). Before he could get another word out, Pete replied, 'I don't know what to say, mate, shit happens. Do you know where Eileen keeps the pepper?'

During the meal Jim and Pete got into a heated dispute about football. 'You never listen to anyone,' Jim was shouting. Pete was protesting equally loudly that he *did* listen.

Before Pete left that evening, he said to me, 'Sorry about that. Don't know what Jim's got such a cob on about.' When Jim left, he said to me, 'Sorry about that, but that guy really winds me up because he never listens to anyone.'

The moral of that story is that you don't have to give advice or offer solutions. Just listen and offer a bit of support. A simple, 'Sorry to hear that, mate,' from Pete would have made all the difference.

Skill 2: the ability to express yourself

We live in a competitive society with increasing pressure to keep up with the demanding pace. When friends ask how we are, the standard reply is often, 'I'm fine', even when we're not. It's as if we think any reply to the contrary is a sign that we can't cope or are not good enough.

Without meaning to, you can get in the habit of holding back and not expressing how you *really* feel. However, good friends are not there to judge you or see it as a sign of weakness when you're not feeling fine. Being honest and open about your emotions is the stuff that bonds friendships. If you're choosing the right friends, then you're safe to be yourself and express yourself freely. Here are some little goals to try.

Little goal: identify any feeling and emotions you are not able to talk to a friend about You may find that you are able to talk about anything. However, if there is stuff you can't talk about, you need to think about what's stopping you or why you are fearful to express yourself. Unless you are choosing the wrong friends, you are doing yourself and your friends a disservice by not revealing and letting them get to know the real you.

Little goal: remind yourself of all the qualities your best friend has A best friend should be someone you can trust and rely on, a person who can keep a confidence and be there when you need them. If your best friend has all the right qualities there is no reason not to express yourself.

Skill 3: the ability to be appropriate in a conversation or situation

With close friendships you may well find there are no subjects that are off limits. However, tact and timing play a big part. There may be subjects that a friend would not appreciate being brought up in the company of others, and always trying to set the tone of a conversation will not go down well. Here are some useful little goals to keep you on track.

Little goal: be aware of the company you are in When you're in the company of a close friend, it can be easy to overlook other people who are present. Be careful not to make them feel excluded, and remember that some subjects are fine to discuss in private with a friend, but they may not want them made public. For example, they may have a good laugh with you about a dodgy date they had, but if you mention it in front of others they could feel you have betrayed a confidence.

Little goal: pay attention to the nature of a conversation and the general mood There may be subjects you want to discuss, but there are some good guidelines to follow. These are:

- Make sure you are not always dominating or setting the tone of a conversation.

- Think about whether or not this is the best time to discuss a certain subject.

- Would the subject you want to discuss bring the mood down or up?

- What you discuss with a friend on a night out over a few drinks may be very different from the conversation you have over coffee on a Monday morning.

Skill 4: having both self-awareness and an awareness of others

I have a friend who will sometimes say to our group of friends, 'Excuse me, can we talk about me now?' The comment always goes down well because my friend is both self-aware and aware of other people in the conversation. When we all get together there are quite a few very talkative individuals (myself for one) and strong-minded people in the group. Having the group attention and being the topic of conversation is a real treat and we all love the attention. So it's fine to flag up a request for it.

However, a friend who occasionally requests attention is very different from the friend who constantly demands attention. While there are self-esteem issues at play with attention-seeking behaviour, it is also an indication of a lack of awareness. Here are some useful little goals that will tell you if you need to work on this skill.

Little goal: phone a friend when you have nothing in particular to tell them If you only ever call a friend when you want to discuss something, be careful. It could be that you don't pick up on what's going on for them and never bother to call them just to see how they are.

Little goal: have a conversation with a friend where you avoid talking about yourself If you find this easy to do, then you can rest assured that you are not an attention seeker or someone who always dominates conversations with your issues. However, if you really find this little goal difficult it's a sign that your focus is only on your own issues. Keep practising until you break the habit of always talking about yourself.

Skill 5: respecting other people's feelings and opinions

Refraining from personal criticisms and personal comments is a very good indication that you are respectful towards others. Avoiding interfering with a friend's problems is also a good indication of respect. When a friend has a problem it's only natural that you want to help. However, don't confuse a helping hand with taking matters into your own hands.

I'll give you an example. Let's say a friend tells you that their boyfriend has been cold and distant lately and they can't seem to find out what the problem is. If you were to approach your friend's boyfriend and ask them what the problem was I doubt very much that your efforts would be appreciated. Interfering in someone's personal relationship is disrespectful, and even when intentions are good it always pays to think how your actions may be interpreted. Try these little goals.

Little goal: practise giving your opinion without sounding as though you are attacking someone else's It's much better to say, 'I think,' or 'In my opinion,' rather than, 'You're wrong,' or 'I don't agree with you.' Giving an alternative opinion is obviously expressing disagreement. However, stating the obvious by actually saying you don't agree with someone or telling them they are wrong sounds much more confrontational.

Little goal: make sure your actions are respectful If you want to help a friend with a problem, think about how you would feel if they acted in the same way.

Skill 6: the ability to recognise the basis of a relationship

As mentioned at the beginning of this chapter, there are different types of friendship. You'll find these little goals useful for determining different relationships.

Little goal: make a conscious effort to remind yourself of the basis of a relationship Ask yourself whether it is a close friendship where you can say *anything* and discuss *any subject matter*. Is it a new relationship where you are still in the process of getting to know each other? Perhaps it's a work-related friendship where certain protocols have to be observed.

My client Louise was having a drink after work with her female boss. After her second glass of wine she thought it would be OK to criticise company policy and petty rules. Her boss cut the conversation short by saying, 'Never drink on an empty *head*, Louise.' Whoops – I don't think any of us would like to be on the receiving end of that scathing remark!

Little goal: make a list of your close friends and the friends you have through association You may know off the top of your head who your close friends are, but it's useful to remind yourself. Sometimes we can become overly familiar too quickly with new friends, or forget how we got to know someone or become associated with them. For example, my client Mel was dating Dave for six months and became very friendly with his friends and their girlfriends.

Case study

Mel's relationship with Dave came to an abrupt end one weekend when he was being bombarded with text messages. Initially he claimed they were from friends, but when they continued into the early hours of Saturday morning, he finally confessed that he was seeing someone else. Worse still, he had introduced her to his friends, none of whom had told Mel.

Mel was devastated by the betrayal. She also felt let down by Dave's friends and humiliated at the thought of them laughing at her behind her back. I told Mel that unless they were extremely unpleasant individuals this would not be the case. It was far more likely that first and foremost they were Dave's friends, and even if they didn't agree with his actions they did not see it as their place to interfere.

Skill 7: having a healthy level of self-esteem and confidence

If you find that you are constantly explaining or justifying yourself to friends, you need to work on your self-esteem and confidence. Additionally, if you found the little goals in skill 4 difficult, you need to work on this area. Here are some little goals to try.

Little goal: take charge of organising an event When your self-esteem and confidence are low, it's easy to sit back and let your friends take charge. However, you'll feel a lot better about yourself if you push yourself to do something you wouldn't normally do.

Little goal: ask a good friend if they think you have a problem in this area When your self-esteem is low you need the support of friends, but at the same time you don't want to put a strain on a friendship by being an attention-seeker, constantly needing reassurance and behaving in a way that alienates your friends. There are times when we don't know whether our behaviour is unacceptable; by talking it through with a friend you can get the support you need and take on board any comments they make.

Case study

Thirty-two-year-old builder Andy told me about the problem he was having with his friend Chris. He said, 'I've been friends with Chris since secondary school. He's always been a bit of a pain when he's had a drink, but recently he's got a lot worse and causes a scene every time we go out. If he's not getting into an argument with someone at the bar, it's the waiter in the restaurant or an argument with his girlfriend.'

Andy had confronted Chris about the problem, and Chris had resolved not to drink when they went out. Not drinking was helping because the following weekend Chris didn't cause a scene, but he hardly spoke the whole evening. The same thing happened the next weekend. While Andy was relieved that there were no arguments or scenes, he was concerned about how subdued and down in the dumps Chris seemed.

Andy finally got Chris to open up and tell him what the problem was. Chris said, 'I haven't got much confidence unless I have a drink. I wanted you all to think Chris can stand up for himself, and that I'm not a wimp. I felt terrible when you told me I was spoiling everyone's evening with my behaviour.'

Chris had made some progress and could see how alcohol actually made him *aggressive* not *assertive* (this is often the case when alcohol is used to combat low self-esteem). However, although Chris had always been the quiet one in the group when he wasn't drinking, he was becoming more and more withdrawn. When Andy described him as 'totally sound and a great mate to have', I suggested to Andy that Chris would really benefit from knowing what his friends thought of him.

I couldn't help but laugh in the next session I had with Andy, when he said, 'It might not be very blokeish, but your suggestion worked. All the lads sat down with Chris, and in turn we told him all his good points. Luckily, the rugby came on before anyone started hugging.'

The support and compliments Chris received from his friends gave his confidence the vital boost it needed. As Andy said, 'It's great having the old Chris back, and even when he has a drink he doesn't make a scene.'

As you can see those seven skills are very useful, and as you go from strength to strength using them your relationships will be stronger.

Filling in your form

Now it's time to turn to the form for this section, for friends/social life. I have completed a sample form to help you. In the development skills section I identify what skills would be useful, i.e. skill 2 and skill 7. You will recall that I did this in the previous chapter, and suggest that when you fill in your form you identify what skills would help you achieve your goals.

Exercise

FRIENDS/SOCIAL LIFE

Goals

1. Be more open with friends about my feelings.

2. Have a fantastic social life.

3. Increase my circle of friends.

Little goals

1. Let my best friend know how nervous I am about starting my new job.

2. Talk to my friends about ideas for new places to go and things to try.

3. Take up a new hobby.

Personal strengths

1. I'm a loyal friend.

2. I'm excited about trying new things.

3. I like the idea of having a variety of different friends.

Immediate challenges/blocks/problems

1. I find it difficult talking about my feelings and always make out I'm fine.

2. I keep finding excuses to put off doing things.

3. I'm not good at making the first move and talking to people I don't know.

Development skills

1. Learn to express myself (skill 2).

2. Organise my time better.

3. Improve my confidence and self-esteem (skill 7).

Achievements

1. I have friendships that have lasted over twenty years.

2. I have wonderful memories of holidays and adventures with friends.

3. I never forget a friend's birthday.

Here are some more big goals that are typically chosen in this section, and some subsequent little goals.

Big goal: get in touch with old school friends

Little goals

Log on to Friends Reunited or a similar website.

Write a letter to old school friends if you have an address for them or their family.

Big goal: make some new friends

Little goals

Join a group or club like a book club or walking and rambling group.

Volunteer for a local good cause – for instance, you can sell raffle tickets door to door for charity.

Put your skills and expertise to use – maybe you could coach the local football club or give lessons in something.

Start your own group: if you have an interest or hobby, get together with like-minded people – whether it's an interest like collecting *Star Wars* memorabilia or playing poker.

Take an evening class.

Big goal: see more of my friends

Little goals

Get out your diary and schedule in some time to see friends.

Call your friends and arrange a night out.

Have a dinner party or barbecue.

Big goal: be more supportive to my friends

Little goals

If a friend has a problem, ask them if there is anything you can do to help.

Take the time to listen to friends and make sure you are not always talking about your own problems.

Be more generous with compliments. Point out friends' good points and all the things you like about them. Remember the difference it made to Chris when Andy and the lads told him all his good points!

Big goal: have an exciting social life

Little goals

Check out what's on in your area.

Try a new restaurant.

Plan ahead so you can make the most of bank holidays and arrange something like an Easter egg treasure hunt.

Try and do at least two different things in the next month, like ice skating, bowling or go-cart racing.

When you have completed your form, make sure you put those little goals in your diary.

Dealing with relationship problems

At the beginning of this chapter I said that friendships tend not to sink under the same pressures, commitments and responsibilities as family relationships. However, we still invest a lot of time and emotions in friendships. They are very important, and we can experience a significant sense of loss and upset when friendships break down.

I'm going to do some trouble-shooting now and look at how to avoid unnecessary misunderstandings, remedy the unavoidable ones and recognise when a friendship has run its course.

Monitoring your reactions

We all know someone who overreacts to every situation. Let's be honest – people like that are a complete pain. You feel uncomfortable in their company because you're waiting for the next drama.

I was in a supermarket queue recently and the man in front of me was kicking off at the checkout girl because he didn't like the music. 'How can you listen to that rubbish? Doesn't it get on your nerves? Doesn't it drive you mad?' he ranted, not waiting or wanting an answer to the questions he was aggressively firing. Then he stormed out of the shop as if someone had committed a heinous crime.

The poor checkout girl smiled sweetly at me, and said, 'What's his problem?' I shook my head in disbelief and thought, *I agree, what* is *his problem?* If people only took the time to think things through before they reacted.

There are times when an overreaction is the result of letting lots of things build up. Then it's a case of the straw that breaks the camel's back, and you find yourself losing it with the wrong person or with the right person but over a minor issue.

Monitoring your reactions and keeping things in perspective is a valuable asset in any friendship and relationship.

Asserting your boundaries

Only you know how you react to a boundary being crossed, and for the most part we can all go with the flow and overlook certain things. However, you have to watch out for the drip, drip, drip effect when you are not really letting something go but instead storing it up in your resentment tank. Once that tank is full it will overflow, and you'll either internalise that frustration by beating yourself up or there will be an outburst in someone else's direction.

The more in touch you are with your boundaries, the better your ability to react appropriately to a situation will be. Friends have had major and permanent fallouts as a result of not recognising and dealing with lots of minor issues. You may have a good friend and feel that something is getting in the way of that friendship. My client Fiona was having difficulty with her best friend. She said, 'I can't quite put my finger on it, but I often feel irritable in her company.' Luckily, and with some help from me, Fiona was able to identify lots of small niggling things that in isolation seemed insignificant. However, as you know from reading this book, doing lots of small things soon adds up to a big thing!

The small stuff does matter. If you know what it is you can nip a situation in the bud before it escalates. Moreover, here's a very good reason to do it: the individuals who are clear about their boundaries and draw attention to them at the appropriate time are the individuals who have the least amount of confrontation in their lives. Not only that, but they also have peace of mind because they're not being churned up over petty resentments and dwelling on what they could or should have said.

Here are some big and little goals that will help you.

Big goal: react in line with your values

Little goal: remind myself of your values

By doing this you will know if someone has really crossed the line. If they have then you're right to draw attention to this. However, remember that you can let a friend know you are unhappy or disapprove of their behaviour without shouting the odds. Stay calm and explain why you are upset. Keeping a level head gives the other person a chance to make amends or apologise, whereas an attack from you will be met with a defensive response or matched with a counterattack.

If a friend repeatedly crosses the line or you believe their actions have really gone too far, think carefully about what you want to happen next. If it's been a close friendship over a long period of time, ask yourself if their actions justify ending the friendship. Is there a time in the future when you think the matter could be resolved? In the heat of the moment a dispute appears black and white. Before you make a drastic decision here are some helpful things to consider.

- You can distance yourself from a friend without terminating the friendship completely.

- If you've already invested a lot of time in the friendship, it warrants investing time in making a decision about what to do.

- People do change and even if you find you have a lot less in common with a friend than you used to, they still may have the qualities that first attracted you to them. Therefore the friendship may not be over, but simply moving to a different level.

My advice is that even if you decide to walk away from a friendship, do it in such a way that you won't have burned your bridges should you want to resume it in the future.

Big goal: be clear about your boundaries

Little goal: write down how many times you feel a boundary was crossed during the course of a day

You may find it difficult to immediately identify what your boundaries are, but if you spend a day paying attention to all those little – what I call – irksome incidents, you'll soon start to recognise your boundaries. It could be someone using your coffee mug at work, your flatmate using the last of the milk again or a friend who is always running late.

Big goal: make friends aware of your boundaries

Little goal: establish a boundary today with a friend

To do this you could stop going along with something you don't like doing, let a friend know you prefer it if they don't turn the music up in your car, or tell the friend who's always running late that it does cause you a problem.

Don't be afraid to assert your boundaries – I really can't emphasise this point enough. If you do it in a courteous way, you won't cause offence or have people dislike you. I'm sure it won't surprise you to know that my friends have a very accurate idea of what I like and dislike. They also know what I will and won't tolerate. And I have it on their assurance (I did check with them before writing this) that they really *do* like me!

In my experience a lot of people would like to be more assertive, but they are fearful of offending others. That's because they confuse being assertive with being aggressive, pushy and a complete pain. Spend a few minutes thinking about the sorts of friends you want to have. Here are some of the problems that arise when a friend can't assert boundaries.

- They keep changing their mind.

- It's hard to gauge when they really like something or dislike it.

- They sit on the fence and won't commit to giving an opinion.

- At times you sense an atmosphere with them but don't know what you've done.

- You would like to think they like you but you're not sure because they treat everyone the same.

- If they do get upset about something you can't believe they're being so petty.

I know it's a hard-hitting list, but the friend who can't assert boundaries is an unknown quantity. If they can't let you know what they really think and feel, can you be sure they'd be there for you in a crisis, stand up for you if someone criticised you and give you support when you need it? The reality is that you never know until that friendship is put to the test. I'm sure that, like me, you'd prefer to know that your friends *do* know where they stand with you. As I said earlier don't be afraid to assert your boundaries.

We've covered a lot ground in this chapter and your hard work should be paying off. Let's see how well you've done by checking your scores in the life chart.

	Low									*High*
Friends/social life	1	2	3	4	5	6	7	8	9	10

SUMMARY

- Having a good friend gives you a great feeling.
- You get to choose your friends.
- There is every reason to have great friends and a great social life.
- Use the seven relationship skills.
- Fill in your form for friends/social life.
- Make sure you are adding those little goals to your diary.
- Monitor your reactions so that you are not overreacting to something or doing nothing when you should be reacting.
- Assert your boundaries.

14.

Improving your personal relationships

I LOVE THE IDEA OF A happy ending and that love conquers everything. However, the reality is that love alone will not guarantee a happy and successful relationship. Both personal and professional experience has taught me that you can't leave personal relationships to chance.

There is nothing random about the people we are attracted to and the relationships we find ourselves in. Every attraction you feel and every decision you make to pursue a relationship is the result of what world-renowned relationship counsellor Barbara De Angelis calls 'personal emotional programming'. If you want to make a relationship work or to find the right relationship you have to understand your personal code.

In this chapter I discuss your personal emotional code. I show you how to make smart relationship choices and how the seven relationship skills can be applied. We look at why good relationships take time, then move on to your personal relationship form and finally give you little goals to enable you to get it right in a relationship.

I've condensed a lot of information and set you some very powerful little goals. It's therefore important that you take your time to work through this chapter, because you may find yourself having to confront difficult issues and make difficult decisions.

However, I promise you it's well worth putting in the effort now if you want happy and successful relationships.

Personal coding

This is a tough nut to crack because you may be both surprised and alarmed at some of the things you discover about the relationship choices you make. I'll explain why. If I were to ask you to describe your ideal partner, your description would probably be of a person who matched you in many ways; someone with very similar values, likes and dislikes, along with similar lifestyle choices. For example, if you are a non-smoker, only drink a minimal amount of alcohol, and like to keep fit and pursue outdoor activities, you would be mismatched with a heavy drinker who takes drugs, abuses their body and has no interest in outdoor activities.

However, many couples are mismatched and even when they describe what they want in a partner they are attracted to the complete opposite. It's not a case of opposites attracting – it has much more do with your personal programming and the unconscious code that is directing you. My client Judy, a thirty-six-year-old physiotherapist, was shocked to discover that the vast majority of her previous partners shared the same negative traits.

Judy wanted an emotionally mature partner, someone hardworking, and responsible, who could talk openly about their feelings and make a commitment to a relationship. Yet she always found herself with work-shy irresponsible men who couldn't talk about their feelings and often had an addiction to either alcohol or drugs.

Your emotional programming is determined early in childhood and acts as an unconscious blueprint. It is not my role or area of expertise to look at what happened in your childhood that determined your individual programming (I do recommend Barbara De Angelis's book *Are You the One for Me?* for an in-depth insight).

However, what I have found when working with clients for the last nine years is that when they uncover negative patterns and their conscious minds become aware of what were previously unconscious negative choices, they are able to confront the problems and make new positive choices.

When Judy listed the negative traits of previous partners she had a revelation. It wasn't just down to bad luck – for whatever reason, she was *choosing* dysfunctional men. With her new found awareness she broke her old pattern and started to make smart choices.

If you have a history of unhappy relationships, listing previous partners and their negative traits is a very useful exercise.

Making smart choices

Begin by making a list of qualities in your ideal partner. Make it as detailed as possible. Include things like:

- What they look like.

- What type of values they have.

- Personal lifestyle choices like drinking, smoking and taking drugs.

- Religious or spiritual beliefs.

- Attitude towards work.

- Ability to talk openly about their feelings.

The more detailed your list is the better. It's important to reinforce in your mind what's important to you and what areas you can and can't compromise on. We are all quick to dismiss a negative trait when we are attracted to someone, but it will come back to haunt you if it's something that really compromises a personal value or belief.

If you're already in a relationship where you are making a lot of compromises and you and your partner are mismatched in a lot of areas, you'll find it helpful to write down why you are staying in the relationship.

Before you make a decision about a relationship, it's a good idea to brush up on the seven relationship skills. These skills help to improve existing relationships, determine the basis of a relationship and attract the right sort of relationship.

Applying the seven skills

Skill 1: the ability to listen

Even if you're a very good listener something happens when you fall for someone. It's not just a case of seeing them through rose-coloured glasses; you may also be *hearing* what you want to hear and putting your own spin on it. That was certainly the case for my client Kim.

Case study

Kim, a twenty-nine-year-old hotel manager, met Liam, a vet, when she took her sick cat Gismo to his practice. She told me, 'The veterinary nurse showed me into the consultation room and when Liam turned round my jaw hit the floor. I stood rooted to the spot staring at this gorgeous six-foot-two vet with tanned skin, blond hair and piercing blue eyes that made my knees go weak. When he asked me what the problem was with my cat, it was a few seconds before I could compose myself.'

Sadly Gismo turned out to be terminally ill with cancer, and after several trips to the vet he was finally put to sleep. A tearful Kim went home alone that day. Later in the evening Liam called her to see how she was. A few nights later he called again, only this time he invited her out for dinner to cheer her up. It was the start of a passionate romance.

On their first dinner date, Kim wanted to know about Liam's relationship history. He told her that his previous relationship had lasted for eleven months and that his ex-girlfriend was, in his words, 'A horrible cow!' Kim *was* shocked by his brutal description. However, she told herself it was out of character. After all he'd been so sensitive and sympathetic towards *her*. For the rest of the evening he behaved impeccably, holding doors open and rushing to help with her coat as they left the restaurant – and when he escorted her home he insisted that she was safely inside the front door before he left.

Over the next few weeks Liam behaved like the perfect partner. He was kind, thoughtful and very affectionate. However, when Kim tried to get more information about the ex-girlfriend his top lip would curl into a snarl, and he'd say, 'I don't want to talk about that horrible cow!' She tried changing tack by saying, 'Things obviously ended badly between you two but as you were together for eleven months you must have some good memories?' If he did, he wasn't sharing them.

Kim convinced herself that as Liam was so lovely on every *other* level, his ex-girlfriend must have been a nasty piece of work and she wouldn't ask any more questions about her. Unfortunately, her opinion of him dramatically changed one evening.

They had arranged to go to the cinema, but Kim had a splitting headache and called Liam to cancel the date. He suggested he'd come round to look after her. She thanked him for the offer and said that all she wanted to do was to have an early night, but she'd call him the next day when she was feeling better. His mood suddenly turned, and he said, 'You never appreciate anything I do. It always has to be on your terms.' Kim replied, 'That's not true.' Then he said it: 'You're nothing but a selfish, horrible cow!'

Not surprisingly, Kim didn't call him the next day or ever again. She ignored all his nasty text and phone messages.

We can all be taken in by a charmer, but you can be sure of one thing – anyone who describes an ex in brutal terms is more than capable of describing you in the *same* terms. Even when you've been on the receiving end of bad behaviour from a partner it's *no excuse* for resorting to derogatory name-calling. Listen carefully to what someone says about their ex-partner. They can tell you about behaviour they didn't like and give you examples of that behaviour without delivering personal insults about the perpetrator. Here are some useful little goals to try.

Little goal: listen carefully when your partner or a new date talks about their ex Make a mental note of any personal insults like name-calling or criticisms of their appearance or of a genetic feature such as the size of their nose and height. And before you say to yourself, they would never say that about *me*, remember my warning – anyone who describes an ex in brutal terms is more than capable of describing *you* in the same way. Also listen carefully to how they describe their own behaviour in the relationship.

Be careful with the 'get out of jail free' card if they say, 'I've changed and I'd never treat *you* like that.' You know I'm a firm believer in people's ability to change, but if they're still slating the ex they haven't changed or moved on from an old relationship.

Little goal: accept what a partner or date is telling you and don't put your own interpretation on it If someone is telling you that they don't want a serious relationship or commitment – believe them. Unless they're a compulsive liar they're telling you the *truth*. If they tell you they were unfaithful in their last relationship, guess what? The odds are extremely high that you're next in line for the same treatment.

Little goal: ask questions Remember how Kim stopped asking Liam questions about his ex-girlfriend? You may think asking your partner or a potential partner questions isn't very romantic, but it's the only sensible way to get to know someone. There's nothing romantic about finding out the object of your desires has a murky past, is a blame merchant or is incapable of having a healthy relationship. You may hear something you don't want to hear when you ask questions, but it's better to find out sooner rather than later.

Skill 2: the ability to express yourself

Some individuals are aware that they find it difficult to express themselves in a personal relationship. It helps to know the truth because *then* you can tackle the problem and do something about it. However, you could be one of those people who aren't aware and thinks you are expressing yourself when the reality is that you aren't. Just because you can sit and talk to your partner for hours on end doesn't mean that you are good at expressing yourself. Your conversation may focus mainly on them and their issues. You could be talking about lots of different subjects but avoiding all the areas that are actually crucial to a healthy relationship.

I want you to study the following list and put a tick next to the things you have been able to express/achieve with an existing or previous partner. Don't be tempted to tick the things you wanted to or wish you had discussed/achieved. Equally, don't tick the things you think you should discuss/achieve with a future partner. Existing and previous relationships will give an accurate indication of where you are really at with expressing yourself.

Exercise

- I have been able to talk about my past openly and honestly.

- I have been able to talk about my family and the relationship I have with them.

- I have been able to talk about previous relationships without slating an ex-partner.

- I have been able to talk about my values and what's important to me.

- I have been able to assert my boundaries.

- I have been able to talk about my feelings towards a person openly and honestly.

- I have been able to talk about my sexual history, birth control and my attitude towards sex.

- I have been able to talk about what I want and expect from a relationship.

- I have been able to talk about love and commitment and my feelings on those subjects.

- I have been able to talk about my needs, wants and desires.

- I have been able to put my foot down when someone has crossed the line or compromised one of my values.

- I have been able to retain my self-worth and sense of personal identity in a relationship.

Expressing yourself in a personal relationships means being able to put a tick next to all of the above – and yes, I really do mean all of them. Don't panic if you were only able to tick a few because I'm giving you some little goals to remedy the situation. Continue working your way through the other items on the list.

Little goal: today you are going to express one of the items on the above list You owe it to yourself to have your needs met and you can never have your needs met if the person you are in a relationship with doesn't know the real you. Continue working your way through all the items on the list.

Little goal: ask your partner if they know at least three values that are really important to you Ideally they should know all your major values. It's down to you to let them know.

Skill 3: the ability to be appropriate in a conversation or situation

I recently heard a funny story from one of the workmen renovating my new house, although it wasn't funny for Dave (as I'll call the workman) when it happened.

Case study

Dave got a phone call on his mobile from his wife when he was at work. She said that one of their fish had somehow managed to jump out of the tank and was flapping around on the sitting-room floor. She couldn't bring herself to pick it up and wanted Dave to come home from work and rescue the fish. The only problem was that Dave was at the top of scaffolding rendering the front of a house. Apart from the fact that he couldn't really leave work, the fish was unlikely to survive in the time it would take for him to get home.

Dave told his wife to stop being ridiculous, pick up the fish and put it back in the tank before it died. His wife screamed down the phone, 'You're useless, you never do anything I ask you to!' then slammed the phone down.

About thirty minutes later Dave saw his wife's car pull up at the foot of the scaffolding he was on. She jumped out, grabbed the scaffolding and started shaking it. Then she shouted, 'See how you like it to have your life put at risk. That poor fish could have died because of you!' Dave told me that his life literally flashed before his eyes and he was so traumatised by the experience that he spent the rest of the afternoon in the pub shaking from head to toe and trying to calm his nerves with a large whisky.

It's a shocking story, I know. Few people would put someone's life at risk because they'd got something out of context (on a monumental scale) and behaved in a totally inappropriate way. Having said that, a lot of people put their relationships at risk by being inappropriate in a conversation or situation and thinking it's OK to turn the tables on a partner. Here are some little goals that help you to be appropriate.

Little goal: always think about what your agenda is In good relationships you can get away with turning the tables on your partner when your intentions are good and you have no hidden agenda. It's fine to have a joke at your partner's expense. For example, I was on my way to a barbecue with a guy I was dating when I missed my footing on a grass verge and went careering into a rose bush. My left cheek was left with three horizontal scratches from nose to ear. My date took great delight in introducing me to people at the barbecue by saying, 'This is Eileen –

she's a self-harm [instead of self-help] expert!' This was a great ice-breaker and got over my embarrassment at arriving with my face looking such a mess.

However, there's a difference between good-hearted humour and using humour as a deliberate put-down or to score points against your partner. Revealing private details about a partner and bringing up issues that are best discussed in private is not appropriate.

Little goal: keep your conversation relevant When couples have differences of opinion they often try and support their arguments by bringing up previous situations. If a situation is relevant then its OK to refer to it, and doing so can shed some light on the point of dispute. What you have to watch out for is sweeping statements like, 'You always say that,' or 'You always do that.'

You also have to be careful about bringing up bad experiences and painful memories. For example, when James's girlfriend told him off for coming home drunk with friends and waking her, he said, 'You're such a killjoy – no wonder your last boyfriend cheated on you.' If James had any reason to believe his girlfriend was a killjoy, he certainly wasn't making a valid point by delivering a cruel and totally irrelevant comparison.

Skill 4: having both self-awareness and an awareness of others

I wonder if, like me, you've been out with a friend who spent the entire time texting or phoning their partner. It's fine if there is some emergency, but as we both know it never is.

When some individuals get into a relationship they seem to lose all awareness of others. Their relationship takes over and common courtesy goes out of the window. As well as a lack of self-awareness they have little awareness of the boundaries they should be observing. Your partner is not someone to keep tabs on 24/7. When you're not with your partner they may be on your mind a lot. However, you can still be aware of everything else that is going on in your life, be actively involved rather than constantly distracted, and allow your partner to have their focus on something else. Here are some good little goals to use.

Little goal: don't use the phone to keep tabs on a partner
Unless your partner is in the secret service or is married (not to you, by the way), you'll have a good idea where they are or the general location they're in. Constant text messages and phone calls are *obsessive* and not conducive to a healthy relationship. It's also extremely intrusive because in short you're trying to invade a person's head-space and have them preoccupied by you. If you think that's a nice idea, think again. Start obsessing about your partner and you're on the road to losing awareness.

Little goal: make sure you are still pursuing your own interests People say they lose themselves in a relationship and in the right context that's OK. You may talk about *losing* your heart to someone, being *lost* in the moment and *losing* all sense of time when you're with that special person. But what you don't want to lose is your mind, friends, hobbies and other interests. Staying rational in a relationship, seeing your friends and pursuing interests outside your relationship keeps your self-awareness and awareness of others grounded.

Skill 5: respecting other people's opinions and feelings

At the beginning of a relationship you only tend to notice all the things you have in common. What many couples do is assume they have a lot *more* in common than they actually do, and this extends to assuming that you both think the same things and have the same feelings. The reality is that you are both individuals and even the most compatible couples won't always share the same opinions and feelings.

Respecting your partner's feelings and opinions is an essential ingredient in a good relationship. Trying to force your opinion on a partner and having no regard for their feelings is an indication of a dysfunctional relationship. Here are some little goals to encourage a healthy relationship.

Little goal: remind yourself that it's not necessary to keep repeating a point It is normal for us to repeat ourselves when someone doesn't agree with us. You may need to clarify what you're saying, give additional or background information, and explain further why you feel a particular way. But in personal relationships there is a temptation to *keep* reinforcing a point or issue. It can be because you feel misunderstood, but the most destructive reason is trying to wear your partner down.

Little goal: remind yourself that respect is a two-way process We can all be quick to complain when someone has hurt our feelings and shown us little respect. However, there are times when your partner's behaviour is a direct consequence of *your* behaviour.

Skill 6: the ability to recognise the basis of a relationship

You would think that when two people are dating or having an intimate relationship they would both have a good idea of the basis of that relationship. Not so – in fact, when you talk to some couples you actually wonder if they're having a relationship with an entirely different person.

Instead of describing the relationship they are actually having they are describing the relationship they *want* to have. I remember walking across a beach last year with a friend and asking her how things were going with her boyfriend of four months. She replied, 'Oh, great, we're really solid.' Then, ten minutes later, I watched the boyfriend of four months totally blank my friend when she walked into the bar. When she rushed over to talk to him he was surly, and he left without even saying goodbye to her.

It won't surprise you to know that they are no longer together.

Just for the record, I don't give my friends advice about their relationships unless they ask for it – and to be honest, nothing I said would have made a difference, because when there is that level of denial going on people don't listen. Until *you* are ready to look at a relationship for what it is at *this moment in time*, no amount of well-meaning friends or family can give you that reality check. Here are some little goals to try.

Little goal: define the basis of your relationship If you are single, you might define yourself as single and happy that way, or single and looking for the right person. If you have just started a relationship or dating, you might define your relationship as being in the early stages. If you have been in a relationship for over six months, answering the questions on the following list will help you to define your relationship.

- Is this an exclusive relationship, and are you are both monogamous?

- Are you both open and honest about your feelings and where you stand?

- Have you introduced each other to your parents and friends?

- Do you feel confident that you will be seeing this person from one week to the next?

- Do you describe the other person as your boyfriend/girlfriend?

- Is there anything or any person getting in the way of this relationship?

- Are you at the stage you want to be?

- Do you feel that one of you is more committed to the relationship than the other?

- Are you describing how your relationship is *now* and not how it used to be or how you would like it to be in the future?

- Does this relationship make you happy? (I'm not asking you if you are really into this person and really want to be with them, but if the relationship makes you happy and if you're getting what you want from it.)

Little goal: match your definition of your relationship with evidence and experience If you define your relationship as being a loving, committed relationship and that's an accurate description, you'll have no problem backing that up with lots of examples, such as 'my partner often tells me how much he loves me', 'she is always supportive', and 'we have made a commitment'.

Remember the friend I walked across the beach with who said her relationship was solid? Imagine how she would have struggled to match her definition with specific examples.

Skill 7: having a healthy level of self-esteem and confidence

This skill is *imperative* to a healthy relationship. Without it you risk getting into a dysfunctional relationship, driving your partner away because they can't cope with your insecurities and avoiding relationships completely.

I want you to look at the following list, which highlights some of the problems low self-esteem and confidence cause.

- You believe you are unlovable.

- You doubt your ability to have a good relationship.

- You think the right person will fulfil your needs, making you feel happy and whole.

- You stay in a bad or dysfunctional relationship because you don't want to be on your own or think you deserve anything better.

- You need constant reassurance from your partner.

- You are jealous and constantly worried that your partner will go off with someone else.

If you can identify with more than one thing on the above list, I suggest you revisit Chapter 5, on boosting your confidence and self-esteem.

We all experience insecurities in relationships and periods of doubt. That doesn't mean you have very low self-esteem and confidence. All you may need is some useful little goals to keep you on track.

Little goal: use daily affirmations This is a great way to boost your confidence and self-esteem with reaffirming statements like 'I love and accept myself'.

Little goal: make a list of all your positive qualities and what you have to offer in a relationship It's not enough to remind yourself in your own mind. Putting things down on paper makes them feel real and is a more solid confirmation.

What to do when it's not working

Out of all the seven life areas, personal relationships is where there is the greatest tendency to set goals that require *other people* to change. I've seen goals 'like make my partner talk to me', 'make my partner spend more time with me' and 'make my partner treat me better'. I've even seen goals like 'make my partner love me'. You can influence your partner's behaviour in the short term through manipulation, but ultimately you can't change them.

Keep a note of your feelings and moods If all is well in your relationship, you shouldn't be feeling anxious, constantly fretting if you haven't heard from your partner, or nervous that you might say or do the wrong thing.

Make sure you are doing things you want to do socially Good relationships involve compromise. You may not enjoy standing in the freezing cold watching your boyfriend play football, or being dragged around the shops on a Saturday while your girlfriend shops until you drop. However, if you are both prepared to compromise and make an effort, you won't feel short-changed or deprived of doing the things you enjoy.

Be on the lookout for fatal flaws You can't fix your partner's problems – only they can. While none of us is perfect, there are some serious flaws that will prevent you from having a happy, stable relationship. They include addictions to substances such as alcohol and drugs – and even addictions to prescribed medication. Addicts themselves are often in a state of denial, but it's important that you're not. My client Amber was in denial about her boyfriend's drinking problem.

Amber told me, 'Martin only drinks at weekends and never during the week.' Unfortunately, his mood would always change for the worse when he did drink, and therefore he *did* have a drinking problem. Just because a person can refrain from alcohol for periods of time doesn't mean they don't have a problem. Drink problems are not defined by the amount and frequency but by the effect they have on a person. Don't waste your time trying to pacify the drinker – the only way to solve the problem is for them to quit drinking.

Other 'fatal flaws' include anger, infidelity, emotional immaturity, control freaks and individuals who are emotionally damaged. If your partner has a fatal flaw they need to get help, because their problem will always get in the way of your relationship.

Remind yourself that however much you love your partner, you must love yourself enough to get out of a bad relationship Trying to solve a partner's problem is as good as saying that you are responsible for the problem, which of course you're not. When you love someone it's understandable that you want to help them, but you should not do so at the risk of sacrificing your own happiness, self-esteem and emotional well-being.

Make sure the pros outweigh the cons Make a list of all the good things in your relationship and all the things you are dissatisfied with. Be brutally honest. I say that because it can be scary seeing this stuff on paper. We are all inclined to kid our-selves that it's not really that bad; that you're just going through a difficult time and things will get better. This may not be the case and you could find yourself having to give your partner a final ultimatum to deal with their problems, or walking away from a relationship.

Regardless of how much effort you are willing to put into a rela-tionship, that relationship will only be successful if the other per-son is equally willing to put in the effort. There comes a point when you have to ask yourself 'What is the likelihood of this rela-tionship improving?' 'Where is the evidence that the person I'm with wants to change?' It's important to look for evidence and not base your predictions on promises. If you feel you have invested enough time and energy in a relationship and things are not going to change, then it's time to move on.

Good relationships take time

Dating can be a minefield. The boundaries normally observed in getting to know someone can become blurred when you find yourself attracted to someone and convinced that there is a strong connection. However, it's important to remember that while physical attractions are usually instant, strong emotional con-nections are built up over time.

Case study

My client Carla was still in the process of divorcing her violent and abusive husband when she started dating Mike. Their first date went really well, and within a week they were having lengthy phone con-versations. Before their second date, she received a letter from her husband's solicitor saying he was contesting the divorce. Mike called later that day for a chat and Carla told me, 'Mike commented that I sounded a bit down and the next thing I knew I was unloading every painful and graphic detail of my marriage.'

The information was clearly too much for Mike, whose response was, 'I don't know what to say.' The next day he sent Carla a text message saying that he was sorry, but he had to work at the weekend. Carla knew that this was the last she would hear from Mike. Initially she felt he could have been more understanding and supportive, but during our session I discussed with her the seven relationship skills, in particular being appropriate in a conversation and recognising the basis of a relationship.

Mike was demonstrating his interest in dating Carla, but he wasn't about to offer unconditional support to someone he barely knew. Carla felt upset that the relationship ended so soon, but recognised that she would be in a better position to find the right partner when she was less needy and insecure. She also learned from her experience that she needed time to recover from her previous relationship.

While you can have physical intimacy immediately, that's not the same as *emotional* intimacy, which is built up over months and years. You can't rush this process, however strongly you feel about someone. And it's worth remembering that lust is easily confused with love. Those overwhelming feelings you experience at the beginning of a relationship may quickly fade as you go through the process of getting to know someone. Equally, they can develop into something meaningful and you may decide that you want to be with a person for a long time, not just the good times.

Imagine meeting a new acquaintance. Think about the amount of information you would share with them on your first, second and third meetings. If a friendship began to form, you would gradually let them into your world. However, when there is a strong physical attraction and the potential for a personal relationship, it's amazing how quickly we all want to immerse that person in our world and become part of theirs. There are ways to pace a new relationship and use little goals to stop yourself from trying to fast-track it. Try the following ones.

Make a list of questions you want to ask a new date/partner

For example you might want to know about their previous

relationship history, their values, hobbies and family background. Rather than interrogate them by asking lots of questions at once, you can schedule into your diary the questions you would like to ask over the next month.

Make sure you are scheduling in time in your diary to do all the things you usually do This might include seeing friends and family, and pursuing any interests or activities.

Set weekly goals of what you want to achieve with a new relationship Seeing your little goals on paper each week will help you to see if they are sensible goals in a new relationship, and if you're not trying to move too quickly. For example, if you set a goal like 'find out what my new date/partner likes to do socially, i.e. eat out, what food they like, the atmosphere or people at a venue', that would be a good goal for week one. On the other hand, a goal like 'introduce my new date/partner to all my friends and family' should stand out as being premature!

I'm going to take time to get to know a person Keep reminding yourself that there's no rush. You may feel as though you've known a person for ages, but you haven't – that familiar feeling is chemistry and the powerful pull of sexual attraction.

I'm going to be careful not to disclose information about myself that will leave me feeling vulnerable Disclosing a painful experience that you haven't recovered from can make you feel vulnerable, especially if the other person seems insensitive or is unable to give you the feedback and support you want.

I'm going to have fun and focus on relaying positive qualities about my life and myself You don't have to be secretive or operate on a need-to-know basis – just avoid having conversations that are dominated by your problems.

Let's look at your personal relationship form now. I have filled in a sample form to help you.

Exercise

PERSONAL RELATIONSHIPS

Goals

1. Communicate better with my partner.

2. Do more fun stuff together.

3. Be more confident and independent.

Little goals

1. Tackle small things when they come up instead of letting them build up.

2. Go to the pub quiz on Tuesday night with my partner.

3. Start using daily affirmations to help me love and accept myself.

Personal strengths

1. I'm committed to this relationship.

2. I value the importance of doing things together.

3. I know that my insecurities are something I have to overcome myself.

Immediate challenges/blocks/problems

1. I often sound as though I'm nagging and complaining.

2. I've got into a rut and never bother arranging to do things with my partner.

3. I keep taking out my insecurities on my partner and constantly need reassurance.

Development skills

1. I need to listen better and learn how to express myself without criticising my partner.

2. I need to be more organised and plan ahead.

3. I need to improve my confidence and self-esteem.

Achievements

1. I have been with my partner for three years.

2. I have learned from the mistakes I made in previous relationships and I'm a lot more level-headed.

3. I have learned to trust my partner and deal with my jealousy.

Other common big goals that are set in this section include:

- Have a loving and committed relationship.

- Spend more quality time with my partner.

- Bring some romance back into our relationship.

- Find the right person for me.

It's important to keep your goals positive so, for example, rather than setting a goal like 'move on from a painful relationship', it would be better to set a goal that identifies what you want to achieve, not what you want to move away from. Therefore a better goal would be 'learn to be happy on my own and enjoy being single'.

Keep setting little goals in your diary that contribute to your big goals. Here are some little goals to help you get it right in a relationship.

- Define what I want from a relationship.

- Make a positive contribution to my relationship every day.

- Plan different activities with my partner.

- Keep my communication with my partner positive.

- If a relationship isn't working decide how much time I am willing to invest in this relationship.

- Make sure I'm not expecting my relationship to satisfy all my needs and I'm still working on other areas of my life.

I said at the beginning of this chapter that I'm condensing a lot of information. It's important for you to allow yourself time to work through this chapter. You can complete your personal relationship chart below, or alternatively revisit this area when you feel you have worked through the goals that are appropriate to your situation.

	Low								*High*	
Personal relationships	1	2	3	4	5	6	7	8	9	10

SUMMARY

- You can't leave personal relationships to chance.
- The relationship choices you make are based on your personal emotional coding.
- Take your time to work through the powerful little goals set in this chapter because you may find yourself having to confront difficult issues and make difficult decisions.
- It's well worth putting the effort in if you want a happy, successful relationship.
- Make smart relationship choices.
- Use the seven relationship skills.
- Use little goals to help you when a relationship is not working.
- If a partner has fatal flaws these will always get in the way of having a happy, healthy relationship.
- Good relationships take time to develop.
- Use little goals to stop you trying to fast-track a new relationship.
- Complete your personal relationship form.
- Use little goals to help you get it right in a relationship.
- Complete your life chart for personal relationships, or alternatively revisit this area when you feel you have had time to work through your little goals.

15.

Living, loving and learning

THE IDEA OF A LIFE HALF lived doesn't appeal to you or you wouldn't be reading this book. You're not planning on sitting down in ten years' time and notching up missed opportunities, reminiscing about regrets and never knowing just how much you were capable of achieving. Your life, like mine, is a work in progress, and it's *essential* to move forward with strategies, goals and techniques that encourage you to live life to the full, which means *not avoiding* any area of your life.

I know from personal experience the consequences of a life half lived. When I was recovering from spinal surgery ten years ago and trying to figure out how my life had got so monumentally out of balance, I was delivered a home truth by a much-loved ex-boyfriend who is now one of my closest friends. He said, 'Do you know what your problem is? You channel all your energies into being successful in business, but make no attempt to be successful in any other area of your life.'

I was all set to retaliate and tell him how wrong he was, but there are times in life when the truth hits you right between the eyes and shocks you into silence. As much as I hated to admit it to myself, he was right. I was good in business, but beyond that I had a string of failed personal relationships, made little time for family and friends, and neglected my health.

Yes, I'd discovered I had a flair for business and got results quickly. But was I really challenging myself or living a full life by only sticking to what I was good at? Of course I wasn't. When I made a commitment to achieve balance in my life and devote the necessary time and effort to other significant areas, there was a question I had to ask myself. Why had I neglected those areas in the first place? It was a tough question to ask and I was shocked by the answers. Low self-esteem was at the root of neglecting my health, and I had come to associate relationships with pain, so keeping a distance kept me safe. There I had it – this bold risk-taker that I thought I was – was taking the safest option.

The safe option isn't a happy one, just an easy one. The real challenge lay ahead and continues to do so, because as I've also discovered, living life to the full means there are always new challenges to face. When you open yourself up to participating fully in life you have to be prepared to deal with the lows as well as enjoying the highs – that's the subject of this final chapter.

Here I show you the benefits and rewards of dealing with the areas of our lives that we find difficult. When you try to block out the bad stuff, you keep the good stuff out. That's why you need to set little goals which ensure that you are challenging yourself in every area of your life, and embracing the philosophy of living, loving and learning.

Living a full life

Everyone has problems – it's how you handle those problems that distinguishes success from failure. Problems can allow us to grow and develop both mentally and spiritually. Without them we might never know our inner strength, wisdom or capacity to dig deep. Problems are a part of everyday life, and while I'm not saying that your life should be full of problems, I *am* saying that to live life to the full involves facing your fears and dealing with problems.

I'm sure you remember how as a child the thought of Christmas or a holiday made you burst with excitement, or how easy it was to have a good wail and cry when you felt sad. Perhaps over the years you've tried to contain or control the difficult and painful emotions like fear, rejection, sadness, loneliness, grief and despair – but inadvertently also diluted the positive emotions. Maybe refraining from having a good cry has limited you from having a good laugh, or fear of disappointment has prevented you from getting excited.

That process of emotionally shutting down can be the result of a bad experience, or just an urge to stay inside the comfort zone.

Case study

Gill, a talented thirty-year-old chef, came to see me when her boss started to complain about her lack of enthusiasm and nonchalant attitude. 'This all sparked off after I had the opportunity of a television slot,' she said. 'It's no big deal – I don't know what everyone's getting so excited about.'

I asked Gill, 'When was the last time you got excited about something?' After two minutes of ums and aahs she said, 'I can't remember.' She was shocked to discover that she really had forgotten what it was like to be excited. In fact she began to realise how many things she turned down or talked herself out of doing. After ten minutes of telling me about the various elaborate excuses and reasons she came up with for not doing things, she said, 'I never realised I was such a negative person.'

I suspected that Gill was actually very fearful and that was the root of the problem. I gave her an exercise to do at home, which was to write on a piece of paper how she felt about doing a television slot and all the emotions she experienced. Gill returned a week later with her exercise completed: the extent of her fears was obvious. Her matter-of-fact attitude masked her fear of disappointing other people, letting herself down and being disliked by the public.

Gill could see for herself that over the years she'd gone to extraordinary lengths to contain her happy and positive emotions so that she didn't risk having to contend with what had become a phobia of being disappointed. I knew we were making progress when she told me, 'I am excited about the television slot. I just couldn't admit it before, even to myself.'

Once Gill had made the decision to do the television slot, she had to go through what I call 'sitting with pain'. Sometimes there is just no getting away from that experience when you are pushing yourself to take on a new challenge or face a fear.

The emotions we all dislike and feel uncomfortable with will present themselves: self-doubt, insecurity and fear of failure. The only way to deal with these emotions and rob them of their power is to experience them and stay on the path you have chosen. In other words, stick with the challenge.

Gill was rewarded for her effort because she handled the TV slot like a true pro. When the producer told her she was a natural in front of the camera, there was a great deal of screaming and jumping around from Gill in the studio.

The emotional scale

The challenge Gill set herself was a big one, but it still required a process of setting lots of small goals to get the big result. I will take you through the techniques I used with Gill and show you how you can gradually build on what I refer to as your emotional scale.

I want you to imagine your emotions as a musical scale. Working vertically down the page in a notebook, list the emotions you usually experience, starting with the positive ones first. Your list might read as follows:

Ecstatic	Bored
Excited	Tense
Happy	Anxious
Enthusiastic	Annoyed
Motivated	Irritable
Loving	Angry
Playful	Rejected
Optimistic	Fearful
Contented	

When you face a fear or new challenge, you often hit every note on that scale. In other words, you experience every emotion. Instead of trying to *avoid* a particular emotion, I want you to see it as *a natural progression and a necessary part of the experience.*

We often do battle with our emotions because we feel that they will weaken our position. Thus you might think that to experience fear makes you weak, but everyone experiences fear. David Miln Smith, author of *Hug the Monster*, has kayaked 2,000 miles down the Nile, trekked the Sahara solo and was the first man to swim from Africa to Europe. He says, 'People think I'm fearless. I'm not. I definitely feel fear, but I have learned through experience how to manage it.'

See fear as not only being *useful* but *essential*. After all, it acts as a warning in a potentially dangerous situation. It can tell you that passing a group of drunk and disorderly louts isn't a good idea, or that taking a short cut through a dark alley isn't the best move. However, it also alerts you to the fact you may need more information, additional skills or more practice until you feel competent. Another bonus is that if you face up to fear, this indicates that you have moved out of your comfort zone and are challenging yourself. You are giving yourself the opportunity to learn, grow and develop. Your aim is to manage fear, not avoid it.

Because we all experience fear it's not surprising that we also fear many of our emotions. This is especially true when we categorise them into good and bad emotions.

Dealing with difficult emotions

However positive we strive to be, or however committed to our faith or spiritual belief, none of us is immune to what are perhaps best defined as the *difficult* emotions. We all feel guilt, anger, resentment, jealousy and hostility. Rather than running from the difficult emotions, you should welcome the message they carry.

The shock factor of a powerful emotion often gets your much-needed attention. A surge of anger will let you know that you feel strongly about something. A flash of jealously might tell you that you're harbouring insecurity. Guilt can be an indication that you regret an action and are learning not to take that action in the future. Feeling hostile can be a reminder of your intrinsic instinct to protect. The emotions themselves are not bad – it's what you choose to *do* with them that counts.

Acting on your emotions

What if you do nothing with your emotions? What if you feel that anger and do nothing with it? You feel angry, but then you feel helpless because you haven't done anything to help. Experiencing difficult emotions can make you feel as though there's a wall in front of you. It's as though you're on a collision course being propelled by the strength of that emotion, and before you crash into the wall you bail out and remove yourself from the situation.

Other scenarios might be: you are under pressure to perform at work, so you throw a sicky; that family get-together is going to bring up lots of issues, so you invent an excuse at the last minute to get out of it; you suspect that you are going to be hurt in a relationship, so you end it before that can happen.

Constantly running away from difficult emotions leaves you having to contend with another set of difficult emotions, like regret, frustration and a feeling of powerlessness. Instead of using difficult emotions as a catalyst to prompt an action (or evaluate a situation), they become something you beat yourself up with. If you walked away from a situation that had made you very angry – you might find that scene haunting you for the rest of the day, or you could feel bad about doing nothing to intervene.

Acting on difficult emotions in an appropriate way allows you to *manage* your feelings and demonstrate that you *can* control what you do with them.

Setting yourself little goals every day helps you to stay in touch with your emotions. A useful exercise to help you find the areas you need to deal with is to keep your notebook at the side of your bed for five days and jot down any emotions you are feeling strongly before you go to sleep. Do the same again in the morning. Look for any reoccurring difficult emotions like feeling anxious, fearful, sad or hurt. Then review the seven life areas on your coaching forms.

Spend a few minutes thinking about each area to see if you can identify what area seems to be triggering a difficult emotion. Perhaps there is a work situation that is making you feel anxious, or a conflict in a personal relationship. Maybe you haven't had much contact with friends recently and need some support or a good night out. It could be that you've been overdoing it and need some time out to relax and pamper yourself. You'll know you're moving in the right direction if you are setting goals that challenge you to do something different.

Challenging your emotions

Of course, difficult emotions can gain momentum in a big life crisis, but they can also get a grip when you slip into inertia. I'll explain how that works. Let's say you've got into a habit of doing the same thing every weekend. After a while your predictable weekends start to become boring, and that feeling of boredom starts to carry over to the rest of your week. Instead of just feeling bored at the weekends, you find yourself waking up most mornings thinking that you can't be bothered with today. That feeling won't go away unless you make some changes to your routine.

Little goals can help you to break your routine. For example, if you always have breakfast at home on a Saturday morning, then get yourself out of the house and treat yourself to breakfast in a smart café or hotel. Here are some other little goals that you can try.

Big goal To make some changes to your routine and do something different.

Little goals

1. Go to the cinema in the afternoon.

2. Visit a museum.

3. Listen to a different radio station.

4. Use a different mode of transport to get to work.

5. Travel to work using a different route.

5. Go somewhere different for lunch.

7. Have a few TV-free nights and read a book you wouldn't normally pick up.

8. Take up a new hobby.

9. Change your social routine – go to a different club or pub, go ice-skating or ten-pin bowling.

10. Join a debating club or book club.

You may have commitments that dictate a certain amount of routine and predictability to your week, but there will still be lots of changes that you can make to add some variety.

What to do in a crisis

What if you find yourself in a major life crisis, immobilised with fear or other emotions like sadness, rejection, grief and a sense of failure? It's a tough call contending with those emotions, and the idea of setting even the smallest goal can seem unthinkable when you're struggling to get out of bed in the morning and feeling like your world has fallen apart. I know that feeling, because when I sat down to write this book I faced the toughest year of my life.

I went through the emotional rollercoaster of a divorce, custody case and my mother being diagnosed with breast cancer. It was a baptism of fire into the breakdown of a marriage, the judicial system of family courts and the anxiety that surrounds the illness of a loved one. Like you, I have no immunity to either problems or emotional pain. What I do have is strategies and techniques that got me through.

When you face a major life crisis there are days when you can only do a little bit, and other days when you have the energy to take on a bit more. It's crucial to have something in sight to aim for, otherwise you may find yourself thinking that you might as well give up now, or questioning the point of everything. Moreover, while you may not be able to get from A to Z overnight in a crisis, you can set little goals that get you from A to B every day. You may have to break down your day into simple tasks. You can convert those tasks to little goals. It can be a goal to get out of bed, get dressed and make breakfast. While daily routines don't cause a problem under normal circumstances, they feel like mighty challenges when you're emotionally devastated.

Major problems can grind you down, making you lose heart or faith. Even when they're behind you, it's not unusual for people to feel jaded and pessimistic about the future. However, as you and I have both discovered, when you set little goals you find that however traumatic the emotional journey has been, you can still retain your zest for life and feel positive about the future. A major crisis can leave an imprint on your whole life, but you can ensure it doesn't take over your life.

Getting through an emotional pounding requires health and stamina. If you haven't the energy to make it to the gym, you can drink a few more glasses of water or use a juicer. Ten minutes quiet meditation can provide a vital recharge. A good cry and some energetic pillow-bashing are both excellent releases. The sympathetic ear of a friend and plenty of big hugs also help to top up your emotional tank.

You never know at what time in your life you'll be called on to dig deep. There will always be those unpredictable events like the death of a loved one, an unexpected job loss and an irretrievable breakdown of a relationship. I want you to remember that if you are willing to do something every day to take yourself in the right direction, you will ride the storm and achieve big results.

Loving and learning

There are pros and cons to living in a small community as I do. Sometimes I miss the anonymity of London (where I used to live), and I could do without the gossip that is prevalent in village life. However, the plus side is feeling that others are looking out for you, being accepted as part of the community and having a re-inforced sense of purpose when your efforts are appreciated.

The heart of any neighbourhood is that section of the community that is able to merge with individuals across the board. That's the part I love and feel I learn the most from, at social events or nights out when I find myself mixing with different characters from a wide range of backgrounds. It's fascinating to watch what appear to be diversely different individuals united by friendship or a love of the sea, or drinking at a particular pub. It's also useful to my work to see how the bonds of friendship and love allow people to learn from each other, as I describe in the following example.

Case study

Angela is a twenty-nine-year-old hairdresser who owns even more self-help books than I do and is always quoting from them (something I don't do socially). She's big on loving oneself and political correctness. It therefore didn't go down too well when Jason, a forty-something DJ, said, 'I've never met a bird who talks about themselves as much as you do, Angela.' Angela threw her head in the air, and said, 'It's derogatory to call women birds; you're obviously not used to talking to women with high self-esteem.' Then she marched off, leaving me with Jason, who said, 'At least I wouldn't chuck my girlfriend out of the car in the middle of nowhere.' It turned out that Angela's boyfriend had done just that after a row the previous night. And what did Angela do with her high self-esteem? She called a friend to pick her up then asked to be dropped off at her boyfriend's, because she said it was all *her* fault and *she needed to apologise*!

We're all prone to a bit of hypocrisy, but I have to say that Jason is right down the centre line in terms of what you see is what you get. OK, he does call women 'birds' and his girlfriend a 'top bird', but he treats her with a lot of love and affection, and constantly praises her and listens attentively to everything she says. He's also active in fund-raising events, and keeps many a local lad on the straight and narrow with his wise counsel. Jason is honest if not always tactful, and does say what everyone else is thinking. Angela, meanwhile, talks non-stop about herself. It genuinely upset Jason that Angela had been abandoned in the middle of nowhere, because despite their differences, Angela is a friend he loves and cares about, and funnily enough she feels the same way about him.

Angela may not have liked what he said, but it sunk in because she said to me later that evening, 'Tell me if I keep talking about myself.' And Jason tried not to keep calling women birds.

We do all learn from each other. That process of wanting to make a connection or be part of a community means that we are willing to be influenced by the people we mix with. Many of the people I know have never read a self-help book in their lives, but they're out there in the community embracing the concept of living, loving and learning.

You don't have to travel the world or be a jet-setter to experience life. Life is taking place on your doorstep.

You can waste days, months and years living your life on the sidelines and complaining about the world you live in. Alternatively, you can make the decision to be one of life's players and go out there and give it your best shot. You can take an interest in what's going on in your community and the people in it. You can dispense with tunnel vision by learning how interconnected we all are, and that making a contribution is a great way to enlarge your experience of life.

To change your life you also have to let life change you. The more you experience it, the more you make yourself part of it, the greater the capacity you have for *real* change. The most discontented individuals I've met in life are the ones who live their lives in a type of isolation. They see life as one-way traffic, and sit back waiting for it to come in their direction. Sadly, they fail to see that unless they're prepared to travel down lots of different roads, they'll continue to experience the same one-way traffic and have the same experiences. To increase your experience of loving and learning, you have to be out there acting in a loving way, prepared to challenge your beliefs about social issues, preconceived opinions and stereotypes.

You can set goals that encourage you to embrace the concept of living, loving and learning. I'm going to suggest some useful little goals that could help you to make a contribution to others and also benefit your seven life areas.

Big goal To make a contribution to the community you live in and other people.

Little goals

Be a courteous driver You'll be appreciated by other drivers, lessen your own risk of an accident or confrontation, and improve your mental health by not being an impatient road-rage driver.

Smile more at people You'll get favourable responses, and smiling helps release feel-good endorphins.

Recycle your litter You get to feel good doing your bit and the planet benefits.

Volunteer for a good cause Check out what's needed in your area: is there an elderly person who needs a hand with the shopping or a bit of DIY? Does the local charity shop need a volunteer? Does the youth hostel need your help? As well as getting to feel good, you'll learn a lot from the experience.

Share your skills and time There must be a friend or family member who would benefit from your skills or time. Don't wait to be asked – offer. Perhaps you could do a bit of babysitting, pick someone up from the airport or help with homework? Putting yourself out for friends and family will strengthen relationships.

Visit your local MP at his surgery If you feel strongly about an issue, you can have your say and find out what you can do to make a difference. The quality of your life is affected by government decisions, and its often local lobbying that influences decisions higher up the ranks.

Give stuff away that you don't need It will help to clear your clutter and you'll feel happier knowing that it's gone to a new home and not the bottom of the bin bag.

Start a support group You don't have to be a trained therapist or counsellor to get together with friends and discuss ways in which you can support each other, whether it's by sitting down together to watch a film and chilling out in company, giving a bit of moral support and sharing experiences, or asking for encouragement to stick to your diet or go to the gym.

Initiate or organise a social event at work My sister and her partner (who are both teachers) came up with a great eating out idea – around the world in eighty restaurants. Every month, staff took it in turns to come up with a different country's cuisine, for example Indian, Chinese or Italian. It strengthened bonds by forging social as well as professional relationships, and they got to be really creative in thinking up new locations to eat at.

Give out more compliments As a rule of thumb, people who give few compliments receive few compliments. Be generous at sharing the positive thoughts you have about others. If your compliments are genuine, they'll sound it and you'll make better connections with people.

Useful hint

Set aside at least five minutes every day to celebrate – think of all the positive things that have happened to you today and all the things you have to be grateful for. Nurture your gratitude and appreciation of life every day, and you'll soon find that celebratory feeling staying with you for longer each day.

Reviewing your spiritual/religious life form

I'd now like you to review your form for spiritual/religious life. If you haven't completed it yet, this would be a good time to do so. This form is optional, and not every individual wishes to explore this area of their life. However, in my experience, every single client I've worked with has a need for a sense of purpose in their life, as do you. You don't have to have a defined religious or spiritual belief to benefit from this form. Having read this chapter you can see that your spiritual/religious form lends itself to personal interpretation.

You can use your spiritual/religious form to set big goals that are in line with your existing faith and beliefs. As an example, big goals could include going to church every Sunday, praying every day or reading from the Koran. You can also set big goals that encourage a more meaningful connection to the world you live in, which I've illustrated in the following completed sample form.

Exercise

SPIRITUAL/RELIGIOUS LIFE

Big goals

1. Discover my sense of purpose

2. Live a full and meaningful life.

3. Make a contribution to my community.

Little goals

1. Define my values.

2. Do more and challenge myself more.

3. Read my local newspaper, find out what's going on and get involved.

Personal strengths

1. When I find a good reason to do something I give it my all.

2. I'm committed to living an authentic life.

3. I feel good about myself when I help other people.

Immediate challenges/blocks/problems

1. I often lack motivation.

2. In the past I've always looked outside myself for answers.

Development skills

1. Learn to trust my own instincts and judgement.

2. Take responsibility for initiating change rather than waiting for things to change.

3. Be more trusting in other people and less suspicious.

4. Stay positive even when I have a setback.

Achievements

1. I've repaired a family rift.

2. I've made the effort to get to know my neighbours.

3. I've made more time for family and friends.

4. I've learned to be more loving and forgiving.

There are lots of things you can do to push yourself further and make your life all you want it to be.

You've stayed with me to the end of this book, and I truly hope you've enjoyed the journey as much as I have. As I mentioned earlier, I wrote this book during the most challenging year of my life. I cried a lot, but laughed a lot, too. Whenever I felt tested to the limit, life had a great knack of showing me that we have no limits. There is always more to learn, and I have no doubt that my own personal crisis gave me new strategies and insights to make available to my clients and readers. I hope that, like me, you feel ready to embrace each new day with a sense of passion and personal commitment.

If you have used just 10 per cent of your day applying the techniques and little goals in this book, your life chart will be looking significantly better than it did when you first completed the exercise in Chapter 1. Let's see how your hard work has paid off.

	Low									High
Health	1	2	3	4	5	6	7	8	9	10
Finances	1	2	3	4	5	6	7	8	9	10
Work/career	1	2	3	4	5	6	7	8	9	10
Family/extended family	1	2	3	4	5	6	7	8	9	10
Friends/social life	1	2	3	4	5	6	7	8	9	10
Personal relationships	1	2	3	4	5	6	7	8	9	10
Spiritual/religious life	1	2	3	4	5	6	7	8	9	10

SUMMARY

- Living life to the full means not avoiding any area of your life.
- Taking the safest option in life isn't a happy one, just an easy one.
- Everyone has problems – it's how you handle them that distinguishes success from failure.
- Living life to the full requires you to experience the whole range of emotions.

- Imagine your emotions as a musical scale, and that when you face a new fear or challenge you often hit every note on that scale.
- See fear as being not only useful, but essential.
- None of us is immune to the difficult emotions.
- Powerful emotions get your much-needed attention and tell you how strongly you feel about something.
- The emotion itself isn't bad – it's what you do with it that counts.
- Setting little goals every day helps you to stay in touch with your emotions.
- Little goals can get you through a major life crisis.
- Getting through an emotional pounding requires health and stamina.
- We all learn from each other. To change your life, you also have to let life change you.
- Set goals that encourage you to embrace the concept of living, loving and learning.

Conclusion

Congratulations!

Setting little goals is now part of your daily routine and you're on your way to achieving those big results.

With a reinforced purpose along with life skills and strategies, you're now experiencing a new quality to your life. You have the confidence to say, 'Bring it on' because you've proved to yourself that you're far more resourceful and a much bigger person than you ever realised you were – a person who has stacks of potential.

You have shaped up on every level, sharpened your mind and taken the time to clarify what it is you want from every area of your life. You are living out your dreams and ambitions by meaningfully pursuing them with a purposeful plan. Never again will a crisis leave you were it finds you, because you've taken control of your life and that stops you being a victim of problems or setbacks.

None of us knows at what point in time life will throw a whole heap of challenges at us. As mentioned earlier, I wrote this book during one of the most difficult times in my own life. However, the mark of success is not how you sail through the good times, but how you overcome adversity. That's why I've always felt comfortable sharing my setbacks with you as well as my successes. I hope you're reassured by the fact that the techniques I offer in this book have been tried and tested first hand!

I'm happy to report that my personal crisis is now behind me, and when your focus in life is on where you are going and not where you came from, you're in the best position to turn a situation around and grasp every new opportunity.

There will always be moments of inner reflection and dealing with painful emotions. That's all part of the powerful process that facilitates real change and personal growth. As long as you are combining contemplation with your little goals, you'll continue to make progress.

And here's some food for thought.

The mind has 40,000 to 50,000 thoughts a day. When 1,000 to 2,000 of those daily thoughts are directed to a goal, it will come rapidly.

So keep thinking about and working on those little goals! Don't let a day go by without achieving a triumph.

Write to me and let me know how you get on. You can contact me through my website www.eileenmulligan.com. I'll keep you informed about what I'm up to and of forthcoming seminars and workshops. I look forward to working with you again in the future.

	Sunday	Monday	Tuesday
Sleeping			
Work (include travel time and preparation)			
Grooming (dressing, etc.)			
Health (gym) Fitness routine			
Cooking			
Family/partner			
Friends/social life			
Housework Laundry			
Errands/school run			
Watching television			
Time to yourself (relaxing, hobbies)			
Spiritual/religious life			
Planning time			
Wasted time (too tired to do anything)			

Wednesday	Thursday	Friday	Saturday

Life Area: _____

Goals

1. _____

2. _____

3. _____

Little Goals

1. _____

2. _____

3. _____

Personal Strengths

1. _____

2. _____

3. _____

Immediate Challenges/Blocks/Problems

1. _____

_____

2. _____

_____

3. _____

_____

Development Skills

1. _____

_____

2. _____

_____

3. _____

_____

Achievements

1. _____

_____

2. _____

_____

_____

3. _____

_____

_____

Index

Alex (client) 43–5
Ali, Muhammad 40
Andy (case study) 191–2
Angela (case study: self-confidence) 63
Angela (case study: self-love and political correctness) 232–3
appearance, *see* feeling and looking good
Are You the One for Me (De Angelis) 202
Awaken the Giant Within (Robbins) 28

Belt, Daphne (case study) 2
Ben (case study) 140–1
body image 4
branding, personal 51–5
    appearance 51–2
    behaviour 52–3
    courtesy 53–5
Branson, Richard 3, 51

Cameron, Eve (case study) 31–2
career, *see* work and career
Carla (case study) 217–18
Carlton TV 3
case studies:
    Adam (work) 165
    Andy (confidence) 191–2
    Angela (self-confidence) 63
    Angela (self-love and political correctness) 232–3
    Belt, Daphne (weight) 2
    Ben (finances) 140–1
    Cameron, Eve (workaholic) 31–2
    Carla (relationships) 217–18
    Dave (relationships) 208–9
    David (work) 157

Gill (lack of enthusiasm) 225–6
    Jack (families) 176
    Jim and Pete (listening) 186
    Joe (family) 182
    Jonathan (business) 50
    Kelvin (work) 154
    Kim (relationships) 204–5
    Lisa (family) 180
    Martin (time management) 78–80
    Mel (relationships) 190–1
    Melanie (personal environment) 115
    Mike (self-worth) 10–11
    Mulligan, Eileen (speaking in public) 32–3
    Rosemary (finances) 140
    Sharon (attractiveness) 125–6
    Simon (self-confidence) 74–5
    Sonia (returning to work) 23–4
    Vicky (switching off) 29–30
    Wendy (time management) 86–7
charmed life 92–111
    attitude for 92–3
    positive belief for 93–5
    purpose for 95–8
Collins, Joan 130
Complete Workout for the Mind, A (Lawrence) 95
confidence and self-esteem 61–76
    encoding of 62
    exercise for 66–7
    role models for 67–8
crises 230–1

Dave (case study) 208–9
David (case study) 157
De Angelis, Barbara 201, 202
diaries 8, 90
diet 132–4

emotions:
  acting on 228–9
  challenging 229
  dealing with 227–8
  goals concerning 229–30
  scale of 226–7
environment, personal 112–23
  adapting, to suit lifestyle 114–15
  defining, organising and main
    taining 113–21
  shared 121–2
  weekly plan for 119–20
Evening Standard 32, 33
  exercise 134–5
  extended family, see family and
    extended family

family and extended family 14, 16,
  17, 170–83
  achievements concerning 178
  appropriateness in 173–4
  challenges concerning 178
  development skills in 178
  exercise for 177
  expression skills in 172–3
  goals for 44, 70, 172–5, 176–8
  listening skills in 172
  need to talk about 182
  others' feelings and opinions in
    175
  personal strengths in 178
  and planning 89
  positive values concerning 46
  problems that can spoil 179–81
  and purpose, attitude, positive
    belief and change 103–5
  recognising basis of a relationship
    in 175–6
  relationship skills in 171–7
  self-awareness and awareness for
    others in 174
  self-esteem in 177
  seven skills applied to 172–7
feeling and looking good 51–2,
  124–38
  attractiveness 125–6
  diet 132–4
  exercise 134–5
  goals for 135
  hair 128

  pampering 132
  skin 126–8
  teeth 129
  wardrobe and style 129–32
  see also health
finances 14, 16, 17, 139–52
  achievements in 150
  assessing 145–7, 152
  challenges concerning 149
  and debt 141–3
  development skills in 150
  exercises concerning 145, 146–7
  goals for 44, 70, 148–9, 150–1
  healthy balance concerning
    144–5
  hiding from problems concerning
    139–41
  organising 139–52
  personal strengths in 149, 150
  planning 89, 147–8
  positive values concerning 46
  and purpose, attitude, positive
    belief and change 100–2
  taking control of 143–4
first steps towards change 34–6,
  68–69
Franks, Lynn 32
friends and social life 15, 16, 17,
  184–200
  achievements concerning 194
  appropriateness 187–8
  basis of relationship, recognising
    190
  boundaries concerning 197–8,
    199–200
  challenges to 194
  development skills concerning
    194
  expressing yourself 186–7
  goals for 44, 70, 185, 186–91, 193,
    194–6, 198–200
  listening 185–6
  monitoring reactions concerning
    196–7
  personal strengths in 193
  and planning 89
  problems with 196–7
  and purpose, attitude, positive
    belief and change 105–7
  respect and others' feelings 189

self-awareness and awareness for others 188–9
self-esteem and confidence 191
seven skills applied to 185–92
values concerning 46, 198
full life, living 224–6

Gill (case study) 225–6
goals:
  breaking down 21
  for a charmed life 98
  committing to, with action 24–5
  diary for 8, 90
  for emotions 229–30
  in family and extended family 44, 70, 172–5, 176–8
  for feeling and looking good 135
  in finances 44, 70, 148–9, 150–1
  for friends and social life 44, 70, 185, 186–91, 193, 194–6, 198–200
  for health 18, 19, 21–2, 43, 69, 70, 135–6
  for loving and learning 231–5
  in personal relationships 43, 70, 206, 208, 209–10, 211, 212, 213–14, 215, 218–20
  for positivity 70, 236–7
  religious and spiritual 44, 70, 236–7
  self-supporting techniques for 11–12
  in seven areas of life 12–15, 36
  for social life and friendships 44, 70, 185, 186–91, 193, 194–6, 198–200
  spiritual and religious 44, 70, 236–7
  in work and career 44, 69, 70, 155, 158–62, 166–7
  writing down 8–11
Groundhog Day 68
Gucci Business Age award 3

hair 128
Harrold, Fiona 32
health 14, 16–17, 36
  achievements in 19, 21, 136–7
  challenges to 19, 20, 136
  comfort with success in 22–3

development skills in 19, 20–1, 136
  goals for 18, 19, 21–2, 43, 69, 70, 135–6
  and looking good 124–38
  personal strengths in 18, 20, 136
  and planning 89
  positive values concerning 46
  and purpose, attitude, positive belief and change 99–100
Hilton, Anthony 33

identity, creating 40

Jack (case study) 176
Jim and Pete (case study) 186
Joe (case study) 182
Jonathan (case study) 50

Kelvin (case study) 154
Kennedy, John F. 24
Kim (case study) 204–5

Lawrence, Richard 95
life chart 16
Limiting Personal Identity (LPI) 26–9, 38
Lisa (case study) 180
looking and feeling good 51–2, 124–38
  attractiveness 125–6
  diet 132–4
  exercise 134–5
  goals for 135
  hair 128
  pampering 132
  skin 126–8
  teeth 129
  wardrobe and style 129–32
  see also health
loving and learning 231–5
  goals concerning 234–5
low expectations 3
Lulu 130

McKenzie, Alec 78
MaCullock, Tina 184
Madonna 38–9, 51
Marathon-runner analogy 2
Martin (case study) 78–80

meditation 97
Mel (case study) 190–1
Melanie (case study) 115
Mike (case study) 10–11
money, see finances
Moore, Demi 66
Murray, Bill 68

needs, meeting of 74–5
Norton, Graham 130

personal branding 51–5
  appearance 51–2
  behaviour 52–3
  courtesy 53–5
personal environment 112–23
  adapting, to suit lifestyle 114–15
  defining, organising and main
    taining 113–21
  shared 121–2
  weekly plan for 119–20
personal identity, limiting 26–9, 38
personal relationships 15, 16, 17,
    201–22
  achievements in 221
  appropriateness concerning
    208–9
  challenges concerning 220
  development skills in 220–1
  exercise for 220–1
  expressing yourself in 206–8
  goals for 43, 70, 206, 208, 209–10,
    211, 212, 213–14, 215, 218–20
  listening skills for 204–6
  monitoring fatal flaws in 216
  noting feelings and moods during
    215
  other people's opinions and feel
    ings within 211–12
  personal coding for 202–3
  personal strengths in 220
  and planning 89
  positive values concerning 47
  pros and cons of 216–17
  and purpose, attitude, positive
    belief and change 107–8
  recognising basis of 212–13
  self-awareness and awareness for
    others concerning 210–11
  self-esteem and confidence in
    214–15
  seven skills applied to 204–15
  smart choices concerning 203–4
  social life within 215–16
  time for development of 217–18
planning your day, benefits of
    86–91
positivity 40–1
  for a charmed life 93–5
  goals for 98
  of others 41–2
priorities 77, 89–90

real you 38–48
  defining 39
religious and spiritual life 15, 16, 18
  achievements concerning 237
  challenges concerning 237
  development skills in 237
  goals for 44, 70, 236–7
  personal strengths in 237
  and planning 89
  positive values concerning 47
  and purpose, attitude, positive
    belief and change 108–10
  reviewing, form for 236–7
  in seven areas of life 15, 16, 18
Robbins, Anthony 28
Rosemary (case study) 140
Ross, Jonathan 130

self-worth and self-esteem 10–11,
    61–76
  encoding of 62
  exercise for 66–7
  role models for 67–8
  symptoms of lack of 64–6
seven areas of life 12–18, 36, 99–110
Sharon (case study) 125–6
Simon (case study) 74–5
skin 126–8
Smith, Will 40
social life and friendships 15, 16,
    17, 184–200
  achievements concerning 194
  appropriateness 187–8
  basis of relationship, recognising
    190
  boundaries concerning 197–8,
    199–200

challenges to 194
development skills concerning
194
expressing yourself 186–7
goals for 44, 70, 185, 186–91, 193,
194–6, 198–200
listening 185–6
monitoring reactions concerning
196–7
personal strengths in 193
and planning 89
problems with 196–7
and purpose, attitude, positive
belief and change 105–7
respect and others' feelings 189
self-awareness and awareness for
others 188–9
self-esteem and confidence 191
seven skills applied to 185–92
values concerning 46, 198
Sogyal Rinpoche 97
Sonia (case study) 23–4
spiritual and religious life 15, 16, 18
achievements concerning 237
challenges concerning 237
development skills in 237
goals for 44, 70, 236–7
personal strengths in 237
and planning 89
positive values concerning 47
and purpose, attitude, positive
belief and change 108–10
reviewing, form for 236–7
in seven areas of life 15, 16, 18
Stephen (school friend of author)
55–6
symptoms of lack of 64–6

talents 55–9
exercises in identifying 56–7,
58–9
teeth 129
Thatcher, Margaret 81
Tibetan Book of Living and Dying, The
(Sogyal Rinpoche) 97

Time Trap (McKenzie) 78
time:
changing 81–6
chart to assess use of 82–3
and flexibility 89
management of 78–91
ordering 90–1
planning 86–91
and priorities 89–90
and saying no 85
for sleep 81, 84
versus self-management 78–81
wasting 85–6
for work 84

values 42–8, 198
being positive about 46
Vicky (case study) 29–30

Wendy (case study) 86–7
Winfrey, Oprah 51
work and career 14, 16, 17, 153–69
achievements in 156
attitude towards 158–61
challenges concerning 155–6
development skills in 156
enjoyment of 156–61
exercise concerning 155
finding 163–8
goals for 44, 69, 70, 155, 158–62,
166–7
happiness and success in 153–69
managing people in 161–2
personal strengths in 155
and planning 89
positive values concerning 46
preparing for 153–4
and purpose, attitude, positive
belief and change 102–3
success and happiness in 153–69

Yale University 9